GRACIOUS MAJESTIE, whom maye God preserve.

THERE SHAL BE IN YE FORENOONE A

Seruice of Thanksgiuinge in ye Churche of S. Luke

—— AND AFTERWARDES ——

A MOSTE MIGHTIE FEASTE

Wille be provyded in ye Highe Streete,

Atte which Manie and Divers Guestes both Olde & Young
shal be Righte Heartilie Entertained by ye Merrie Burgesses,

—— AND ATTE YE HOURE OF TWO BY YE CLOK, ——

YE CARNIVALLE

—— SHAL COMMENCE ——

Inne ye Lower Grounde ye Friendlie Societies and ye Riders upon ye new
and wondrous invention, yclept ye Bicycle, together with other Menne of
prowesse in ye Towne will holde HIGHE FESTIVALLE, and manie righte
joyouse Sportes shal be open for both Younge Menne and Maidens—to wit:

RACES on ye Flatte for ye MENNE—ye BOYS—and ye MAIDENS.

Races with ye Hoopes and with ye Wheelbarrowe—Sacke Races—Ye Tugge of War—Clymbynge of ye Greasie Pole—Races over
manie and mightie Obstacles—Lykewyse Races with ye Egge in ye Spoone—Ye Steeplechase—Races on Alle Foures—and ye
newe and wondrous Race yclept Syamese.

Yesterday's Town: Maidenhead 1980
has been published as a Limited
Edition of which this is

Number   *281*

A complete list of the original
subscribers is printed at
the back of the book

for Phyl.

Tom Middleton.

YESTERDAY'S TOWN: MAIDENHEAD

FRONT COVER: The toll gate at Maidenhead Bridge.

The Bridge with barge horses working along the river bank, the original use of the tow path.

YESTERDAY'S TOWN:
MAIDENHEAD

THE STORY OF THIS PLACE
AND THE MEN WHO MADE IT

BY
TOM MIDDLETON
ASSISTED BY
PATRICIA CURTIS

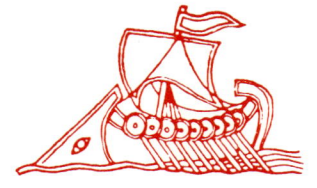

BARRACUDA BOOKS LIMITED
BUCKINGHAM, ENGLAND
MCMLXXX

PUBLISHED BY BARRACUDA BOOKS LIMITED
BUCKINGHAM, ENGLAND
AND PRINTED BY
NEWPAR PRESS LIMITED
BLETCHLEY, ENGLAND

BOUND BY
KEMP HALL BINDERY LIMITED
OXFORD, ENGLAND

JACKET PRINTED BY
CHENEY & SONS LIMITED
BANBURY, OXON

LITHOGRAPHY BY
SOUTH MIDLANDS LITHOPLATES LIMITED
LUTON, ENGLAND

TYPESET IN 11pt TIMES ROMAN
WITH DISPLAY TYPE BY
BRIAN ROBINSON
NORTH MARSTON, ENGLAND

ISBN 0 86023 113 5

CONTENTS

INTRODUCTION & ACKNOWLEDGEMENTS

Only in recent years has the Victorian character of the town of Maidenhead disappeared from the street scene. In the town centre it tumbled into rubble as the demolishers cleared the way for such un-Maidenhead sights as pre-stressed concrete beams, pre-fabricated walls, steel frames, and the assorted underwear of the modern office block and shopping precinct. The country lanes and pathways which had guided people naturally to familiar places on foot were coerced into the confusion of one-way streets, with hazard and danger at every turn.

This seems a good time to record how the framework of Victorian Maidenhead was constructed and to single out a few of the principal characters who had had a hand in putting it together. There are some unexpected parallels between the early Victorians and modern Maidonians. Almost all of them were newcomers. They began with a town centre plan. They met resentment from the locals, and their railway, heavily opposed by vested interests—as was the by-pass in its early days—wrought a comparable landscape change to that of the M4. I have a feeling that the early Victorians would have approved of modern Maidenhead's development, though they would not have understood the social changes.

No book of this sort is produced without an enormous amount of help and goodwill. Most of the material has come from the files of the *Maidenhead Advertiser* which contain a near complete record of the period. In particular, I have drawn heavily upon the *Victorian Recollections* series which was written by Frank Bloomfield; his contribution to the archives is recognised in Bloomfield Road. Without his articles much of the detail of the period would have been lost. Similarly, late Victorian Maidenhead was extensively photographed by George Gude whose pictures turn up all over the place. They form a large section of the Library's collection to whom they were presented by his daughter, Mrs Margaret Pitcher.

One group of pictures was kindly lent by Miss Edith Upson, whose family had much to do with the Maidenhead now disappearing. Mrs Monica Chambers kindly lent another group published here for the first time. They were taken by her grandfather Charles Banwell who was the master at Norfolk Park School. John Brown, who has done extensive research into his family, is another who has added to this record. Victor Moll kindly lent notes prepared by the late Archibald Greenwood Watkins. I must also thank Don Seal, Editor of the *Advertiser,* and Ron Cordon, managing director, for the facilities which they have provided, and Barry Lawrence, Chief Librarian at Maidenhead, who incidentally began the local history collection there.

Patricia Curtis, who is in charge of the Maidenhead Reference Library, has been my collaborator throughout, particularly with pictures, and my old colleague Mike Taylor of the *Advertiser's* photographic staff has produced many excellent copies from old photographs and has advised on reproduction.

KEY TO CAPTION CREDITS

B	Barton	JB	John Brown
BCM	Benson Cycle Museum	MC	Mrs M. Chambers
E	Edith Upson	MAS	Maidenhead Archaeological Society
	PR	Phyllis Radjuschko	

The two bridges which brought most of the invaders.

ABOVE: Peace along the Cliveden Reach. BELOW: Eel bucks. Their wicker baskets made from Thames osiers were lowered to trap the eels.

ABOVE: Ives Place where the Town Hall now stands and seen here when converted to an hotel with tennis lawn, and BELOW: a punt moored on its lake.

ABOVE: Queen Street before the traders got there. (Drawn by the late M. Ernest Andrews) BELOW: The Grand Avenue at the Duke of Westminster's seat—Cliveden.

12

ABOVE: Botany Bay above Boulters, and CENTRE: the house that followed Ray Mill and became Boulters Inn and the island a municipal park. BELOW: River Road.

13

ABOVE: The old White Hart Inn which stood on the site of Cresset Towers. It could stable 50 horses and was an overnight stop for coaches. BELOW: Braywick Arch before the station but with Wethered's coal yard seen here receiving a delivery.

ABOVE: The old Town Hall. Originally there was a market beneath it where bloater sellers and others sold their wares. BELOW: Craufurd College, built by J.D.M. Pearce and demolished in 1949.

THE INHERITANCE

Steam brought coaching Maidenhead to a halt in the early 19th century. The era had lasted only about 100 years, during which time it had turned Maidenhead into a staging post on the Bath Road—a street of inn-keepers benefitting from the activities of the highwaymen on the Thicket. Apprehensive travellers, as the shades of night began to fall, filled the beds of the inns, and the purses of the landlords with gold. Most of the people in its one busy street were going somewhere else, giving it a cosmopolitan air. It was a small place. In 1826 it consisted of 192 houses and 945 inhabitants.

The first hint of a major change in its life style came in 1833, with the publication of the prospectus of the Great Western Railway Company. The company's first terminus west of London was to be at Taplow. A railway undercover man had been busy round the inns and stable yards counting the coaches, noting the people on the move and generally assessing probable custom for the new mode of transport. He reported that Maidenhead was an important travel centre, receiving 70 coaches and other through vehicles daily. He must have rubbed his hands at the prospect of transferring all this business to the permanent way, while perhaps dwelling upon his small part in bankrupting the inn-keepers. But there were other entrepreneurs looking over his shoulder, who would turn the street of inns into a Victorian High Street of private traders, and then energetically develop a community which would spend its money in those shops.

About this time also the two Maidenheads began. The industrious shopkeepers who were to be the backbone of the new community gradually left their cramped quarters above their shops to collect in the new housing estates on Castle Hill and in Norfolk Park, as prosperity came their way. There they fostered a new middle class and set about building their churches and schools to entrench the morality they were spreading.

The other Maidenhead was beginning down at the riverside, where until now only young lads went to fish and bathe. It was wide open for exploitation, with the new link to London in prospect. Thus it was no coincidence that also in 1833, the former head waiter of the Sun Inn, the famous coaching house at the bottom of what was then Folly Hill—he was previously postillion to Lord Cottesloe—made an important purchase. He bought the Orkney Arms, a little inn near Maidenhead Bridge. (In 1743, Maidenhead Corporation had leased to John Marsh a strip of land on the Bucks side of the Bridge to make a way to his inn from the Bath Road.)

His name was William Skindle. He had recently left the Sun to take his first house, the Saracen's Head in High Street. It dated from Charles II's day. He had married the niece of the Sun's landlord and set up as an innkeeper, coach and fly proprietor. Jonathan Bond, founder of the boat business of that name, followed him as proprieter of the Saracen's Head (Marks and Spencer now stands on the site) which became known as the Corporation Arms.

It was when William applied for the licence, and was asked by the bench for the name of his new hotel that a member of the public is said to have whispered 'Why not call it Skindles?' Skindle senior and junior, but mostly junior, were to turn the hotel into the legend that it became in Victorian and Edwardian days. The little Orkney Arms was

rebuilt in the image of the Sun, to become better known than the railway station which made the enterprise possible. It was largely responsible for the development of Maidenhead and the Upper Thames as a fashionable resort. Skindle senior retired at the age of 60, in 1876, and moved to Worthing, where he ran a marine hotel for 30 years, dying in 1917 at the age of 101. Among the famous who were to wine and dine at Skindles were Edward VII and Queen Alexandra. But while the seekers of pleasure travelled on Brunel's railway to Skindles and Thames-side, others followed for business reasons, and so the two Maidenheads became established.

There was, of course, opposition to the changes in the town's life style from all who fed upon the passing trade, not forgetting the Corporation, who were busy misappropriating the funds from the toll bridge at the river crossing. To meet the competition, having lost their appeal against the railway Bill, they reduced the tolls from £18 to £4 on stage coaches—mail coaches with broad wheels crossed free as their heavy wheels acted as road rollers—but they lost the battle to the new middle classes. These Victorian traders were a sturdy lot. They built the town and made most of their own building materials, to become the Men of Maidenhead whom we remember. They were to hold it as a fortress against further change until the Welfare State and the Development Age arrived, when, like the coaches before them, they would hand over, with no more good grace than the inn-keepers and the Corporation did, to the next era. This beginning of our present town, while Mr Skindle was teaching people to enjoy themselves down by the river, turned it into a place where people came to stay from choice. It began amid the meadows and orchards, and it was along the main road through these green places that the first early warning of change came in 1835 in the shape of the noisy *Erin,* a steam coach plying between Marlborough and London. It frightened horses and heralded the end of an era.

When the Victorians began the transformation of the old street of inns there was no police force to keep order, no gas for lighting or heating, an enormous number of beggars, tramps, and doubtful characters whom, no doubt, the end of coaching had thrown out of work on the Thicket and other shady places. Workhouses were full and ratepayers began calling for reforms in local government, which was a bit of a closed shop. Just before Victoria mounted the throne, the Poor Law Amendment Act set up boards of guardians to manage workhouses, and the Municipal Corporations Act extended the franchise among ratepayers. The new shopkeepers, who were primarily responsibe for turning Maidenhead into a settled place, were soon serving as guardians and councillors and began turning their attention towards the organisation of more respectable institutions and services. But on the whole, they were a thrifty and cautious lot, who saw little profit for themselves in noble public acts. This sort of behaviour was left to the gentry who rarely paid their bills with alacrity. So it was that the Men of Maidenhead who began the new town, bringing regalia and uniforms to dignify their civic affairs, set a new style of life appropriate to the merchantry. None was a merchant prince but many were ambitious, solicitous in their shops, cautious in their counting houses, and above all, well-mannered in their dealings. Everyone aped his betters, including the poor. Thus was influence transferred from the big house to the cottage.

Earl Russell who besides being a member of the gentry was also a member of the Maidenhead Board of Guardians, reported to his colleagues in 1897 that he was shocked

to discover that 40 tramps at the workhouse had only eight towels between them and that six or seven men were expected to bathe in the same water. His Lordship's criticisms were not well received. Mr E. Hewitt said they did not want to make gentlemen out of the tramps. Mr G. Lowe, astonished apparently by the Earl's pleading, said he knew of a man who had not bathed for 40 years. If they were not careful they would have to provide nightshirts next. The Guardians, as a compromise, promised to provide as many clean towels and as much clean water as possible but added that each tramp could not expect a clean towel and bath all to himself.

Professional classes joined the shopkeepers. Lawyers and bankers, so essential to the wheeling and dealing of commerce, moved in. Private banks opened and the cash made in the town centre began to flow into bricks and mortar. There was profit in town expansion, as the community began to consolidate. Writers who came down on the railway from London sang the praises of the riverside. William Morris was particularly complimentary about Cliveden Woods, and in a small way we became quite well-known. But Maidenhead remained almost a closed community—you still had to pay to cross the river through the toll gates until the 20th century. Many of the families who had a hand in creating Victorian Maidenhead and in building both its houses and its reputation—'are you married or do you live in Maidenhead?'—are still here.

Their inheritance was an abundant countryside bringing naturalists to live here. The Thames was full of fish, (even a few salmon were left) and there were at least four fisheries formerly owned by the Crown, at Maidenhead Bridge, Upper Garston Eyot, Hamerden Ash (Amerden Bank), Down Place and Ruddle Pool near Bullocks Hatch, all along the Bray Reach. At least one town clerk—William Berry Far—was among local collectors of butterflies. Young boys bathed in their birthday suits just above the old mill at Bray and in other secluded river spots, among osiers, iris, meadow sweet, forget-me-nots, water mint, water lilies and many other wild aquatic plants. The word 'hatch' incidentally meant a gate. Bullock's Hatch translates into the family of Bullock who had an estate near this hatch.

To the north of Kidwells were the Maidenhead Common Fields, originally extending to 368 acres and including the North Town Fields. By 1845 the Enclosure Acts had whittled them down to 290 acres in 217 lots among 17 smallholders. A large part of this area became known as Norfolk Park when building began. To the south and west were orchards, including Louches or Lee's Orchard (Courtlands) which adjoined a large stretch of land called The White Horse. It seems likely that the White Horse public house—it was an inn more than 400 years ago—took its name from this area. Bray court Rolls explain: 'In the year 1600, Robert Winch of Lobrook, yeoman, conveyed to Richard Powney of Bullock's Hatch, and to Richard Winch of Shoppenhangers, yeoman, all that tenement &c lying in Maidenhead called The White Horse, bounded by the highway from Reading to London on the north, and the land formerly John Staverton's now Thomas Terry's on the South, and by the land formerly William Blakemore's on the east, and the highway from Maidenhead to Braywick on the west ...all of which the said Robert W purchased by deed bearing the date 17 April 36 Eliz of Richard Wormstone, of Maidenhead, innholder'.

Deacon's Meadow stretched along Thames-side almost from the Bridge to Bray, over-

running the old archery ground of Old Field. When it flooded and froze, it was a skating ground. When dry, Maidenhead Excelsior Football Club played there. Farm lands, where the Romans had grown corn and where smallholders now grew crops and grazed their animals, rolled away to Furze Platt where town folk went to pick blackberries. There was only one house, Fernley, Captain Fitzmaurice's establishment, between the Robin Hood and the Ram's Horn and Snuffers (Craufurd Arms). Durrant's Meadow, with a five bar gate opposite Park Street, provided a drill square for the Rifle Volunteers with their Enfield muzzle loaders, later replaced by the Martini Henry pieces, a practice ground for the Fire Brigade, and a place to play football of cricket.

Town life outside the inns as the age of Victoria began, centred round the market place. There was no Queen Street; Braywick Road ended at the foot of Folly Hill. There was no Grenfell Road, only Shoppenhangers Lane wandering up the hill, to be diverted when the railway came. The old Manor of Ive sat in rural tranquility where the Town Hall now stands, its fish pond fed by a stream and its extensive grounds breached by Canal Lane, which was to become York Road. The Town Hall was one of the town's newer buildings. The old Guildhall, much smaller, which also contained accommodation for the Town Sergeant, was pulled down. James Payne, town clerk, bought the lot for £100. It is notable that one of the builders of the new town hall was John Cooper. The new building took in a larger site.

Kidwells Manor, with its attached farm lands, dominated the town. The yews in the centre of Castle Hill Roundabout mark its one-time front entrance. They grew in the old Manor House garden. Other family houses of the upper middle classes were Monkendens in the middle of High Street (now Woolworths), the Wilderness, and The Cedars in Bridge Road. The Cedars is currently the Alder Valley 'Bus Depot, but in the 1870s it was the home of Sir George Cooper, ADC to the Viceroy of India. Ray Lodge, a fine old 18th century house, stood in isolation near the river, a creek carrying a stream through its grounds from Widbrooke. There were brambles on the river bank and clumps of thorn bushes. A rope rail was erected across them to carry the barge towing ropes clear. Horses hauled the barges along these public rights-of-way—the towpaths—which in many places were to be stolen from the public by riparian owners. The Thames Conservators, set up to protect public rights, winked their eyes at this singular larceny. A few horse-drawn barges were in use until the 1920s.

In addition to the two toll gates at the Thicket and Bridge, there were gates in Braywick Road (King Street), Oldfield Lane, Forlease Lane, Ray Lane, North Town, Widbrooke, and Pinkneys Green. Their principal purpose was to stop animals straying from one parish into another, where they would be impounded.

It was in June 1838, that the first invaders arrived at the gates of the town in some strength. On that day the *North Star* brought 1,479 people to Maidenhead on the first train to arrive at the old Taplow Station. A week later coaches were queueing at Maidenhead Riverside, as the station was called, to be loaded onto the permanent way for the last stage of their journey to London. Maidenhead was never again the same.

In the year that followed, hundreds of navvies—the navigators who had previously dug the canals—spread their Irish accents through the bars and public places. They had come to change the geography of Maidenhead. With picks and shovels they built the railway

embankment, mutilated and diverted Shoppenhangers Lane, shut out the view towards Windsor, and, on their way to Twyford, left a changed landscape in their wake. Nothing comparable was to happen to the area until the coming of the motorway.

Brunel's railway also brought employment and the beginnings of prosperity for some local people. Charles Batting, whose descendants still live in the area, who had taken over the foundry near Marlow Road Corner from Bullstrode and Rogers, built all the bridges which carried the railway across the lanes. The firm became well-known agricultural machinists. It adapted to change within the embrionic municipality which was developing behind the enclosing wall of the railway embankment. Edwin Rogers of the former foundry also adapted. In 1884 he bought a poultry farm at Furze Platt where Cooper & Son built him a laundry. When he died in 1889, his son Frederick, aided by his brothers Edward and Hezekiah, continued the business which became the Maidenhead and District Laundry in 1906. Today it is one of the town's oldest family-run businesses and is managed by Mr M.F.H. Rogers and re-styled Clean Linen Services Ltd.

The present railway station was eventually planted in the middle of an orchard. The embankment became a barrier which shut out rural Bray and helped to dispel the truth that the town was largely in the old parish of Bray. But in spite of its new status, the area between High Street and Braywick Road was largely meadow, criss-crossed by footpaths. One ran across Cullern's Meadow. We know it as Cullern's Passage. Thomas Cullern was mayor in 1793. Little shops in High Street, hanging on to another age, had bow windows with crown glass panes. The streets themselves were dusty on dry days and muddy when it rained. Alderman Hobbis was reported as saying: 'Those who use Sunday for its legitimate purpose, trudge through the dust, hot tired, and thirsty, to church.' On a windy day the dust rose in clouds and settled on everything displayed in the shops. At such times the tradesmen looked out anxiously for the water cart which lumbered down the street and over the main roads several times a day. On moonless nights one encountered dim figures carrying candle-lit lanterns. Road conditions remained bad for many years. In 1895, a young man called Greenwood Watkins, who worked in the High Street pharmacy (later taken over by Mr Barnes, father of Mr Rickford Barnes of Queen Street), had acquired a penny farthing bicycle. He afterwards wrote: 'It was nothing, suddenly to find a fairly big stone in the way of one's narrow solid tyre, or to pick up a small flint on the tyre which jammed the spoon brake and sometimes threw one off'.

There was no local newspaper until 1869, when the *Advertiser* was founded, but there were crying stations about the town. One was at Top Town Pump, near the present High Street Methodist Church, where the Town Cryer made important announcements, such as proclamations and poll results. The last of the breed was Mark Taylor.

Victorian tradesmen gradually took hold of the town, permeating its government, arranging its education, setting up its institutions and clubs, and, wherever possible, taking a profit on the deal. They even formed a company to bury the dead—the Maidenhead Cemetery Company—when the churchyards began to fill up.

There were, of course, a few families whose lineage reached into the deep past, notably the Langtons who ran the town's major brewery, and the Silvers who were around in the 16th century. But it was the newcomers, we call them the Victorians, who were the driving force in the building of a memorable Maidenhead.

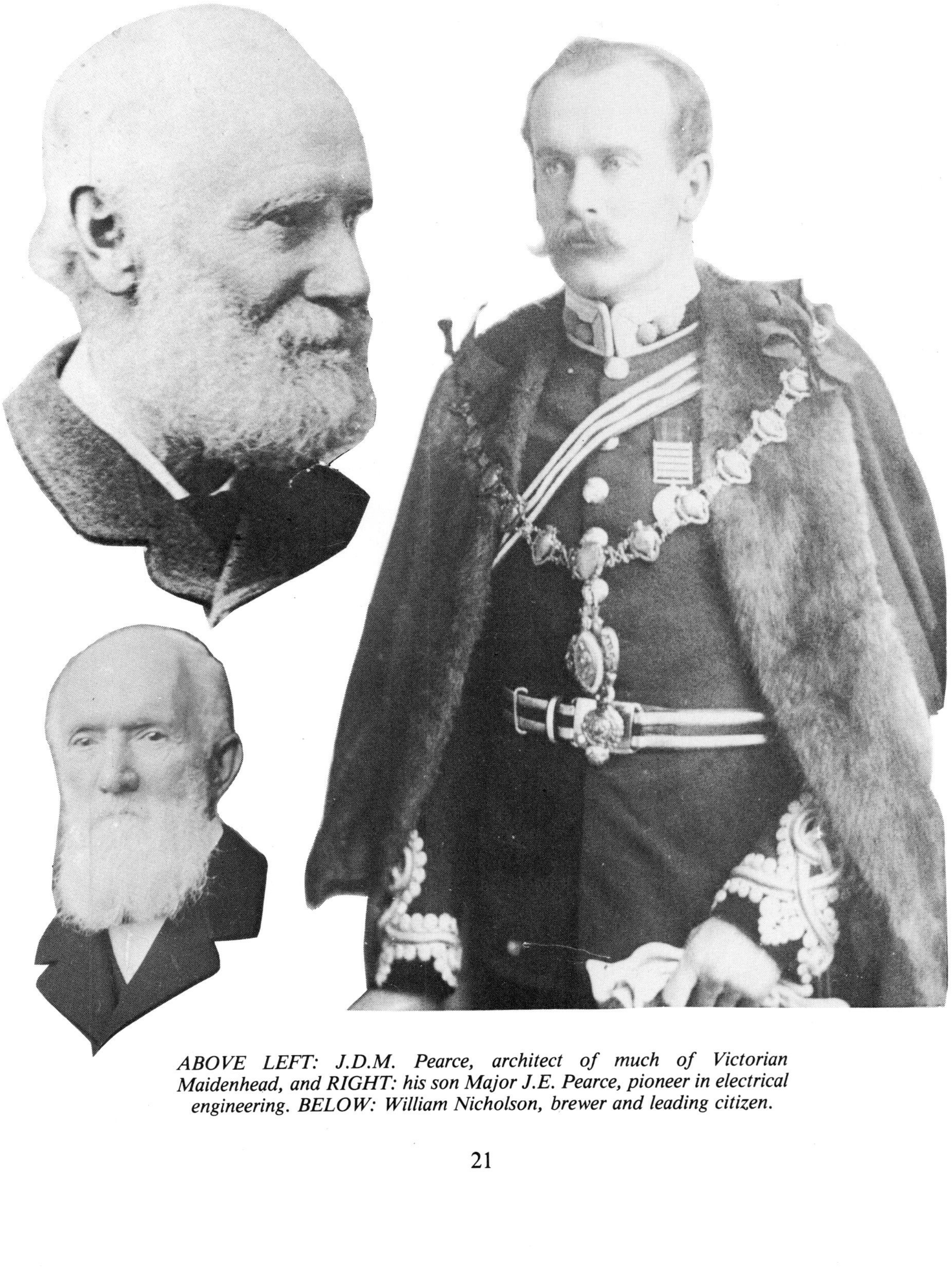

ABOVE LEFT: J.D.M. Pearce, architect of much of Victorian Maidenhead, and RIGHT: his son Major J.E. Pearce, pioneer in electrical engineering. BELOW: William Nicholson, brewer and leading citizen.

ABOVE LEFT: Alderman Richard Silver, a founding father of Maidenhead, who dug up a Roman villa. RIGHT: Alderman J. Wesley Walker, son of Robert, first chairman of the Library and Museum Committee and local historian. BELOW LEFT: Mark James Taylor, last of the town criers, and Borough Mace bearer (1864-1922). RIGHT: Alfred Cull, hatter of the 60s. His business continues as R.G. Bott.

ABOVE: Lower High Street, the Swan Inn and Cull the hatters. BELOW: Two views of Garden Cottages estate, built by Pearce, showing first concrete walls.

CORPORATION STAKES,

To be Run on Tuesday, Nov. 1, 1881

LATEST BETTING.

Probable Starters and Jockeys.

HORSES.		JOCKEYS.
The Three-year-old Mare	- - -	The Turk
Craufurd Wire	- - - -	Bob Nichols
Foxey	- - - -	Young Huntum
Poor Barks	- - - -	Young Martingal
Draper Dealer	- - -	General Jack
Done Brown	- - - -	Jack Smyth
Retired Scorer	- - -	Bill Brighton
Boatman	- - -	Jack Bung
Fussy	- - -	Edwin Greenside

...e are sorry to hear that Fussy is obliged to have Greenside as Jockey, Bloomy being laid up with the gout.

What a bad thing it is for some of the horses going lame over the beautiful path from the Moor Arches to the Bridge. Ask the Boatman about it, the Bungman.

The Three-year-old Mare, [the dearest Mare we ever had, wetted the Chain with Champagne last Friday night, and we hope it won't rust. What does Charlie Box think?

LATEST FROM LITTLE BRIGHTON.— The Scorer's trainer finding the sea breeze too strong for his constitution, ordered him to return to the High Street Mile, where he is in for a digging canter.

If the Fussy horse had not had an extra drink on Saturday night his wind would have been much better.

Judge - - - *Alderman MaKie.*
Starter - - - *Mount Ephraim.*

The Strait Tip may be had of Tont O'Gath, the Painter, King Street.

ABOVE: Another view of Highfield Lane bridge. LEFT: An engraved trowel presented to the Mayor after the laying of the first stone of the new Railway Station, May 1871. RIGHT: Waltham Signal Box, (1891).

ABOVE: The controversial toll gate at the Bridge, c1890. CENTRE: Growing popularity of the river brought new boathouses and commerce. Bonds had a prime site near the Bridge. BELOW The Riviera Hotel, with the headquarters of the Maidenhead Rowing Club adjoining the Bridge.

Two views of East Street, opposite Kidwells Park which has now disappeared.

ABOVE: Cullern's Passage, once a field path from Braywick Road to High Street. BELOW: This was Hine's Yard off Bridge Street. Hine's Meadow car park is now on part of the attached property. INSET: Charles Butler, the poor man's friend. He built Butler's Stores.

ABOVE LEFT: Patriarchal types, as were many Victorian shop keepers, ran Symmons & Son, complete house furnishers and auctioneers at 27 High Street. RIGHT: Where some of the poor people lived in Brock Lane. BELOW LEFT: Mr and Mrs George Gude (he took many of the pictures in this book) in the ornamental gardens which they made at the Hippodrome, Chapel Arches, and RIGHT: Hippodrome, Chapel Arches.

ABOVE: St Mary's and lower High Street from Chapel Arches, and CENTRE: Chapel Arches before the Colonnade. On the right is the present British Legion Club, formerly a common lodging house built by J.D.M. Pearce. LEFT: White Hart Lane in 1906, with Stuchbery's Stores (left) and Hews, cutlers, furnishers, and electricians (right). RIGHT: Walker's the chemist's at the corner of Park Street.

[ESTABLISHED 1869.]   **[ONE PENNY.**

Important Notice.

MESSRS. R. WEBSTER & SONS
Have been appointed Sole Agents in this district
for the

CELEBRATED MOLASSINE MEAL,

which is a Staple Food for Horses, Cattle, Sheep, Pigs and
Poultry.   MOLASSINE MEAL replaces an equal quantity
of meal, cake or other food.

Over 100,000 Tons were sold last year.
Samples and full particulars obtainable at their Depôts.

*ABOVE: Advertisement for R. Webster & Sons, and BELOW: Steane &
Co, King Street. Their successors, the Barton family, are in the Precinct.*
(B)

32

ABOVE: Bridge Street with the Moor Tavern on the right. CENTRE: Leading to Bridge Road, c1906. BELOW: Bear Hotel, just after the turn of the century, and Butler's Stores on Courts' site.

ABOVE: Outside the Town Hall when Martin's the drapers were next door to the bank, BELOW: but in 1881, Martin's site looked like this.

*ABOVE: Castle Hill when a horse could graze on the grass bank, and
BELOW: Castle Hill from High Street.*

ABOVE: James Rutland of Taplow, excavating the site of the Roman Villa discovered by Alderman Richard Silver on Castle Hill in 1886, showing the hypocaust, or fire hole, and the foundations. (MAS) BELOW: A municipal group.

ABOVE: Edwin Rogers left his High Street foundry to open a laundry at Furze Platt in 1886. The buildings went up on a former poultry farm. It is still under family control as Clean Linen Services Co Ltd. It now operates from Maidenhead, Marlow and Reading, and includes a textile rental service. BELOW: Delivery vans before the motor car, c1906.

ABOVE: All Saints buildings at Boyn Hill. BELOW: Opening of the main drainage works by Mayor William Withnall in 1893.

38

LEFT: The J.D.M. Pearce Memorial in Kidwells Park. RIGHT: Benjamin Hobbis, secretary of the committee of library supporters, announced at the opening: 'Henceforth Maidenhead and the British Empire must be governed by what are called the working classes. A reading room giving all information and opinions upon the political, social, and industrial questions they have to decide, is a first necessity for the peaceable settlement of disputes'. How wrong he was. BELOW: Interior of the original library, built by C.W. Cox & Sons. Maidenhead people raised more than £1000 towards the cost.

These old billheads dating from 1801 (Thomas Fleet) disp[lay] the elaborate calligraphy of early printers and engravers a[nd] give a taste of the style of trading as well as an insight into t[he] showrooms. Thomas Fleet's business was taken over by To[m] Stuchbery who had come here some years before to join [his] Uncle James. John Higgs (established in 1825) founded t[he] Methodist movement. Robert Walker became his partner. [He] was a chemist and dentists' selling horse and cattle pate[nt] medicines, paints, lamp oils, wines and cigars. Walker was [a] leading teetotaller! Another billhead advertises spices, f[ish] sauces, perfumery. The address is given as The Market Pla[ce.] Joseph Gurney, in 1860, was selling 'all kinds of hot air a[nd] steam apparatuses'. Baths were made or lent on hire and [all] kinds of old metals were bought. He was also a fine pl[umber] maker and brazier.

The Cookham Union

JOSEPH GURNEY,

Ironmonger,

Tin Plate Worker, Brazier,

COPPERSMITH

Locksmith & Bell Hanger,

MAIDENHEAD.

STOVE, GRATES, & IMPROVED KITCHEN RANGES, MADE & REPAIRED.

All kinds of Hot Air & Steam Apparatuses fixed on the most improved principles

Wind Guards, for the cure of Smokey Chimneys.

FINE LAMP OILS.

All kinds of Baths made & lent on Hire.

KING STREET, MAIDENHEAD.

The Guardians of Cookham Union   July 6   1881

Dr. to H. STEVENS,

COACH BUILDER.

PATENT AXLES CAREFULLY CLEANED, WASHERED AND OILED.

35, High Street,
Maidenhead

Cookham Union

TO A. UPSON,

[LATE WALKER & SON.]

Dispensing Chemist.

MAIDENHEAD   Sept 29th 1889

The Guardians Cookham Union—

W. H. HEYBOURN,

CHINA & GLASS MERCHANT

CHINA & GLASS REPAIRED & RIVETTED.   TERMS CASH.   CHINA & GLASS LENT ON HIRE.

5 Per Cent Interest Charged on all overdue Accounts

To Goods as per A/c Rendered   £ 1 11 5

The Guardians of the
Cookham Union   Sept 30   1889

Dr. to W. BLOWFIELD,

Whitesmith, Locksmith and Bellhanger,

SMITH AND FARRIER,

THE PRIZE KITCHENER

All kinds of Copper Kitchen Goods Tinned and Repaired.

Sole Agent for Haine's Improved System of Gas Lighting.

GAS, HOT AND COLD WATER FITTER, TINMAN AND COPPERSMITH

WEST STREET, MAIDENHEAD.

Residence:—5, ALBAN PLACE, WINDSOR ROAD.

Open and Close Fire Kitchen Ranges Supplied and Repaired, and New Boilers Fitted.

1889

Dec. 31   1888

Mr Chalson

DR. TO G. CARTER,

Saddler and Harness Manufacturer,

HIGH STREET,

MAIDENHEAD.

HORSES AND COWS DESTROYED AND REMOVED.

NATIONAL TELEPHONE NO. 0113.   TELEGRAMS: "HEWS, MAIDENHEAD."

The Cookham Rural District Council   March 31st 1903

Dr. to **JAMES HEWS,**

General Furnishing and Builders' Ironmonger,

WHITESMITH, LOCKSMITH, BELLHANGER,

FENDERS & FIRE IRONS.   Gas & Hot Water Fitter,   TOILET WARE, &c. &c.

HIGH STREET, MAIDENHEAD.

ALL KINDS OF TIN, ZINC, IRON & COPPER GOODS MADE TO ORDER.

CHIMNEY PIPES, COWLS, &c.

Tin, Iron, Zinc and Copper Rain Water Spouting and Piping.

AGENT FOR LEAMINGTON RANGES

Estimates for all kinds of Work.

BAR IRON MERCHANT.

Maker of Plain and Ornamental Fencing.

Any error in this account must be advised within seven days of date, or cannot be allowed at settlement.

1902

Telegraphic Address: "Stuchbery's Stores, Maidenhead."   Telephone No. 13.

63, 65 & 67, High Street, MAIDENHEAD,

Sept 30   1904

The Guardians of Maidenhead Union

Dr. to STUCHBERY'S STORES,

(P. & S. THOMPSON, Ltd.)

Any error in this Account must be notified within SEVEN DAYS of its receipt, or no allowance can be made at settlement.

Furnishing & General Ironmongery,
China & Glass, Bedstead & Bedding
Departments.

41

MEN OF PROPERTY

One of the people looking at the possibilites Maidenhead offered for speculative development, now that the railway had arrived, was Benjamin Cail. Curiously there is no memorial to him in Maidenhead. He lived in a villa overlooking Kidwells Park. A surveyor, designer, and draughtsman, he was one of a small number of people to consider the potential if the town was carefully stimulated towards growth, with suitable rewards for one and all.

At this time the surrounding land was owned by a few local families in fairly large parcels. One name on the plans was R.A. Ward. He lived where MacFisheries now stands in High Street. He had set up a legal practice here, and in the early 1870s became one of the more dignified town figures as Clerk to the Board of Guardians and later magistrates' clerk. He was also perpetual commissioner for the taking of oaths from married women. His firm continues today as C.R. Thomas & Son, solicitors. The whole of the Norfolk Park area, from Kidwells to Cordwallis Road and from Cookham Road to Marlow Road, along with an acreage in the Ray Park district, was marked down to him. Thomas Micklem, whose family lived at Rose Hill, Hurley, owned land north of Cookham Road towards Harrow Lane. Two large areas between the Wycombe branch line and Marlow Road, also a fair acreage in Cookham Road, on part of which the Catholic Church was built, were owned by J.D.M Pearce. These formed the nucleus of the Maidenhead Improvement Company which bought the eight or nine acres where Queen Street, Broadway, York Road, and Grove Road were built. Their plans were not well received by the population who called them 'the Land Sharks'. High Street draper Caleb Coleman became associated with the company. Whether his activities had any bearing on his election campaign for the council is not known. But the opposition put about the following rhyme: 'We'll hang old C on a sour apple tree as we go marching on'. There were obvious parallels between Victorian public opinion and the opposition to the Town Centre Plan of the 1960s. It was the putting into operation of the Cail Plan by the Maidenhead Improvement Company that turned Maidenhead into the country town which it was to remain for almost a century. Pearce himself became an alderman and mayor and for a time acted as honorary town surveyor.

Others besides this company began smaller speculative operations and to back up all this disturbance, local builders, notably John Kinghorn Cooper and William Woodbridge, whose firms took the major share of the construction work, left indelible marks on Victorian Maidenhead. Cooper's decorative terra cotta work, tiles in Pinkneys Green clay, scrolls, and mouldings of all kinds, can still be seen and recognised as his work. The leading modeller at his kiln was J. Handwell. He is generally credited with the design and manufacture of all the intricate tiling work on the former Queen Anne House, which used to stand at the bottom of Castle Hall, and for which Charles Cooper was the architect. Woodbridge had brick fields where what remains of Princess Street stands. The area around it was once known as the Brickfields. His son Frank went into brickmaking at Holyport. Woodbridge built Princess Street and adjacent cottages with bricks made on the site. He eventually covered a huge area of Maidenhead.

The first major change in the town centre came when the demolishers arrived outside three High Street properties: the former Hand & Flowers, Edward's china shop, and Hawker's bread and biscuit bakery. They knocked all three down. The construction of Queen Street followed, with the building of a new terrace as far as Clark & Senior's former premises. These premises (Nos 25/29) were previously William Woodbridge's builders' workshops. But the plan to continue into Ward's Meadow beyond was held up, and the derelict area awaiting the arrival of the builders became regarded by the locals, especially the children, as a common. They called it Queen Street Green. Fairs and entertainments took place there. Of the smaller speculators, Henry Timberlake, a pioneer in the manufacture of bicycles, ploughed his profits back into local property. He also created a good deal of local employment. He built a new terrace on the other side of the Green. Its first occupant was Alfred Starling, who had three claims to distinction. He was the town's first scientific dentist, to use the phrase current at the time, the father of Maidenhead's amateur theatricals, and one of two men credited with the introduction of tennis to Maidenhead. His partner in this latter exploit was another man who was to leave his mark in bricks and mortar upon the growing town. He was E.J. Shrewsbury, the architect. He designed many churches in and around Maidenhead, the Technical Institute, Marlow Road, and the Jubilee Clock Tower. A Thames barge owner named Kingston moved in next door to Starling. That house became the *Maidenhead Advertiser* office, the *Advertiser* moving from its original works in the Broadway, now occupied by architects North & Partners. Timberlake went on to build a 'cycle factory.

Changes were taking place near the river also. Ray Lodge Estate began to be broken up. The Corporation bought a strip of it to improve the entrance to Ray Mead Road. A river wall along Ray Mead Road was also being constructed at this time. This was the beginning of the Promenade. Substantial properties began to appear in Ray Park Avenue, and a rich widow named Annie Smith, who was to become an integral part of the legal history of the town, bought The Fishery on Bray Reach. It was her involvement with certain men of property which brought about the building of the Fishery Estate, following a long legal dispute over the right to fish in the Thames, a right formerly held by the Crown.

Annie Smith, good natured and vivacious except perhaps over fishing rights, became a riverside personality. She gave annual feasts, prepared by Mr Spindler, for the poor. A Christmas party for 300 children was held under a banner bearing the earnest wish of all present and their parents 'God Bless Mrs Annie Smith'. Everyone was not on the good-time band-wagon. Poverty stalked the back streets of Victorian Maidenhead.

When Mrs Smith moved in, The Fishery was the only building on Bray Reach, apart from a boathouse on the mud osier island. To the north of her property, between the house and the Sounding Arch—Brunel's famous bridge—was a large aviary which included a pond stocked with water fowl, among them Black Persian Swans. She was looked upon as a bit of a Bohemian and was not averse to calling her gardener, her boatman-engineer Alf Fitzgerald, her agent, her architect, or others, to her bedroom to discuss the day's arrangements. It is not recorded whether John Kinghorn Cooper ever made the trip but he did make the distinctive entrance pillars to the estate in terra cotta. Each was surmounted by a crest bearing a heron with a fish in its beak. He also added a smoking room to The Fishery. No-one had issued any health warnings about smoking

then. Ladies were just taking it up. In the lower strata, regular smoking concerts were held in working men's clubs, although the more puritanical strongly disapproved of the weed and made speeches about its dangers. J.D.M. Pearce was convinced of its calamitous consequences. Addressing the Anti-Smoking League in 1894, he told them, 'Smokers have dark muddy complexions which are often transferred to their children who are thus cheated out of being good looking'.

Building began on The Fishery in the 1890s opposite Orkney Cottage. Dorothy's Bungalow, Dick Russell's Nest, and Lady Scott's cottage were among the first buildings. They were not regarded as architectural masterpieces. Two redeeming features of the new estate were West Court, built for the architect West Neve and no doubt designed by him, and Bray Lawn, which was built for the popular actress Mrs Russell Potter. West Neve went on to design Bray Village Hall.

Joseph Henry Clark, who lived at Altwood, Tittle Row in the early 70s, developed the top of Castle Hill when the construction of Grenfell Road began, and built Lowood (Lynton House School) where he lived until he died. But undoubtedly the most popular of all the speculators was Charles Butler. In 1863 he bought the premises of Joseph Gurney in Lower High Street. The Gurneys were a well-known local family of traders, fine block tin craftsmen, braziers, locksmiths and ironmongers. In the 1870s William Gurney made the principal parts of a machine for producing gas from petroleum, invented locally by Mr Bloomfield. It was manufactured by Vaughan & Brown of Hatton Garden and one was installed at Canon Hill to replace the coal gas works there for domestic lighting. The family had several businesses. Charlie Butler went on to build on Ives garden what was to become one of the town's first department stores, much on the lines of an early Marks & Spencer establishment. He set out to serve the working man. He found work for the less well-off, built houses they could afford in Cordwallis Street, Denmark Street, Reform Yard, and Waldeck. He also had a builders' merchants' business in Bridge Road where half-inch matching could be had for 7s 6d a square. Three-quarter inch was 10s, and flooring 12s a square. It was cash and carry, no deliveries. In his men's outfitting shop the working man could get a pair of boots, a suit and a shirt for his back, all at reasonable prices. He also built Butler's Hall on derelict land at the corner of Queen Street and Broadway. It let at a cheaper rate than either the Grand Hall (formerly the Hamblettonian Hall and now Sainsbury's) or the Town Hall.

It was during all this development that J.D.M. Pearce, busy building on Norfolk Park discovered that beneath it lay Thames Valley gravel. He used it to make concrete. Concrete walls appeared all over the Norfolk Park Estate and he also built what were believed to be the first concrete houses there, earning himself the title, The Concrete King. His Garden Cottages Estate, demolished after World War II, (Evenlode now stands on part of it) was the town's first estate of artisans' cottages to have inside water—they were built back to back.

Meanwhile, in the High Street, the coaching horn so frequently heard in this narrow defile, slowly gave way to the motor hooter. In the '60s, children would rush into the street as the four-in-hands arrived at the Bear, where the occupants, driver and footmen were refreshed, or to see the pleasure coaches of the '70s, with Captain Blyth or the Marquess of Ailesbury handling the ribbons. Both were gentlemen coach drivers. The

Marquess, who owned the Savenake Estate, ran a coach from Hyde Park to Oxford and back. This reached Maidenhead about midday. For several minutes beforehand policemen were busy ensuring that no cart, truck, or hand barrow, as were used for trade deliveries, impeded its progress. Following the early warning from its coach horn, the coach, crowded with top-hatted men (and occasionally their womenfolk) would clatter into the street, His Lordship on the box, dressed in the approved fashion. The buttons of his greatcoat were reputed to be spade guineas. He was adept at overturning small vehicles in his path. Having done so, he would throw a coin to the person in charge, and go on his way, laughing. Blyth was a captain in the Yeomanry.

On high days and holidays, out of the Bear's stable yard would come long, large pair-horse brakes with black lined yellow wheels. Families would hire them to attend meets of the Royal Buckhounds at the Coach and Horses (now Shire Horse) on the Thicket, or to attend meets at Redstone Farm, Hawthorn Hill. In later years these last were often attended by Edward VII who would travel to Maidenhead by train with his horse boxes coupled to the rear. He piloted many a lady over the fences.

There was excitement also in watching the Night Parcels Mail thundering down Folly Hill to wheel into Marlow Road and then turn sharply into West Street, where it would unload in a great bustle at the post office, kept by Charles Cleare, the town's popular postmaster. From the Red Lion, just below Market Street—it was there in 1663—a variety of traffic would emerge through its old gate entrance, over which the upper storeys were supported on oak beams. For some inexplicable reason the house has been rechristened the Boar's Head. The gatehouse was demolished in 1935. The entrance was large enough to accommodate four-in-hands, stage or mail coaches with all up entering the yard beyond. When an American called Hinton became the landlord in the 1880s, he would drive out in a lightly built racing gig, sitting on the single seat behind the bobbed tailed nag. He was a sporting gent. There was, of course, plenty of horse traffic about, including Richard Illsley's waggons and carts. They coped with the town's carrier business until the motor car arrived. Horse cabs, jarvies and growlers clip-clopped the cobbled streets until the age of petrol. Private carriages brought the ladies to town to shop, their coachmen often lashing shop windows with their whips to attract the shopkeeper's attention, while hoity-toity madam sat becalmed in the leather upholstery.

Another Victorian sight, especially for small boys, but certainly not for madam, was behind Mr Hinson's the harness maker's in High Street. There could be seen Mrs Hinson, a mangling expert, working a huge box mangle, weighted with large stones as she processed the sumptuous linen, removing all suspicion of creases. There was horse trade also outside Hannah Carter's where fine saddles and harness were made. The family business, now in King Street continues the tradition of excellence.

Victorians also encountered a variety of street smells, especially on dipping days at Robert Nicholson's the grocers, later Budgens, and currently rebuilt as Waterglade House. Nicholson's made rush lights for a farthing, tallow candles and dips. Close by, abutting Popes Lane—Brock Lane is all that is left of it—was a pig market, an area of mire with an aroma all its own.

Street noises were different too. Itinerant traders had their own cries, but none so loud as James Ruff the High Street fishmonger. It was said that his 'Mackril-O!', called out at

Littlewick Green, could be heard on Castle Hill. Also, there were gentler street sounds of hop-scotch, made by little girls in pinafores with frilly tops, hopping the chalk frames drawn on pavements, as they edged the flat tile over the lines and into the homes with their laced boots and shoes. All were airborne in street and alley. As to the shops themselves, branded goods were unusual or unheard of. Packaging in our modern colours had not arrived in the mass. There was a blue bag for currants and sugar in universal use among grocers, and many tradesmen employed their own craftsmen in workshops at the back, who made many of the goods sold over the counter. Shopkeepers and their staffs were expert tradesmen and of course the customer was always right. Long before the arrival of non-drip, paints were mixed by colourmen to the customer's requirements, plumbers cast their own sheet lead, and it was not unusual to see bunches of rosemary, gathered from Maidenhead gardens, being taken into No 79 High Street to be received by Mr Rumball the hairdresser. He was a patriarchial figure with a long grey beard. In his shop window was a magnificent wax bust of a lady with beautiful hair. Mr Rumball distilled the rosemary to make perfumes and hair washes. Rumball's son Ted ran a gents' shaving saloon. His other son, Louis in 1869, was a steeplechaser of some note, and took part in the famous race with Mr Timberlake on the Thicket. It was the first race between a cyclist and a pedestrian. H.J. Timberlake, described as a velocipedist, rode one of his own cycles. The stakes were £10 a side. Louis Rumball won.

But changing times eventually brought different demands upon even such trades as blacksmithing. These craftsmen, through their knowledge of metals, began making new products. Sam Tucker of King Street became a link man between the age of the blacksmith and electricity. He was a craftsman who worked for Mr Stubbs the ironmonger of High Street. The building is there, still bearing a medallion on the upper storey. He it was who collaborated with Henry Timberlake in the 1860s. In a kitchen in Albert Street he helped him to assemble the first boneshaker. Thus began the Timberlake bicycle industry, which grew to large proportions here, employing many hands, who in the early days earned threepence an hour. The industry created a demand for houses. It was followed by the Pilot Cycle Company who set up a production line in the former Hamblettonian Hall.

Thomas Timberlake founded the company in 1867. Among other things it produced a twist-grip cable brake acting on the rear wheel, antedating this development in the cycle industry by some 50 years. The business closed in September, 1962, the last of the line being Cecil Timberlake. The brothers built 85 and 87 Queen Street and established workshops there with stove enamelling and plating plants. Their machines won many awards at the National Sewing Machine and Cycle Exhibition in 1887, especially for their diamond-framed safety 'cycle. Originally they built velocipedes to order for £4 10s, progressing to the side-by-side sociable tricycle. They even made a six-man machine which was gold plated for a London newspaper. Henry toured the UK on his machines. Among their many innovations was the *Kangaroo*, a free-wheel device for penny farthings. On October 5, 1890, the Timberlake Brothers began their famous long ride from Queen Street to Edinburgh carrying 20 lbs of luggage each.

Timberlake's first boneshaker had wheels of wood, iron tyres, and pedals cranking directly to the spindle of the front wheel. He also experimented with a mono-cycle, but

this one-wheeled machine did not take on. Timberlake began hiring boneshakers out from his home. The Royal District Cycle Company managed by A.C. Hickling, later opened premises in Grenfell Road and became Hickling & Co.

About 1872, Sam Tucker made the first electronic alarm clock heard in Maidenhead, and his employer Henry Stubbs brought out the first double pole indicator movement. Tucker wound the armatures for the magnets in his little King Street workshop. But the business got too big for Stubbs, and Patterson Cooper of London took it over. Patterson was a local man who had studied at Craufurd College, where Headmaster J.D.M. Pearce was interested in electricity and magnetism and experimental science. Edward Patterson became a pioneer in electrical instruments, and his firm made the first telephone switchboard for Cardiff. Blacksmithing of a high order took place in King Street at James Leaver's Metal Works, next door to the Prince Albert. This firm turned out the most exquisitely beautiful work in ornamental iron and brass. Its foliated scrolls and strap work were a sheer delight. Leaver's leading colleagues included Messrs Barford and Norkett, who later carried on the business. They worked for churches and cathedrals all over the country, and were responsible for the ornamental iron work at the Law Courts in the Strand. Their excellence was in ecclesiastical brass.

Craftsmen of another kind also worked in King Street at Manlove & Taylor, the carriage builders. There they built carriages for four-in-hands, tandems and pairs. Artists painted the crests and rich coats of arms on the backs and on the door panels, the finishing coat of varnish giving the whole a mirror-like glaze.

Shops, on the other hand, often had a character of a different kind. One such was Stubbs the ironmonger. He was a little shrivelled old man who emerged from a deep dark tunnel of iron and gadgetry to stand behind his high counter, which served to emphasise his lack of stature. Children would go there for a pennyworth of gunpowder 'to blow up mum's copper'. Apparently it was an excellent method of clearing away the soot. H. Stubbs would weigh it, screw it up in paper, and caution his young customers to be sure Ma secured and barricaded the furnace door. His shop was stocked from floor to ceiling with all the things that had collected there over the generations. There were candlesticks and snuffers, rush light holders, standard table lamps which burned Colza or sperm oil. Paraffin was only just appearing on the market. Although matches were in use, Stubbs still sold tinder boxes with flint, steel, and tinder, gophering irons, goose and flat irons of huge dimensions, and there were bundles of crinoline hoops suspended from the ceiling. All about was a glorious medley of pumps of all kinds, Dutch ovens, and general hardware. Most of it was still there in the 1980s.

Next door were the coopers and basket makers. They made barrels for Nicholson's brewery, which had no cooper in its early days. On a more social plane, tobacco was becoming fashionable. Smoking was fast superseding snuff taking. Thomas Graham opened what was probably the town's first smoking parlour in 1897 at 91 Queen Street. The gentry collected there to indulge in Graham's fine imported cigars, to draw on his Meerschaum pipes, and perhaps inhale Graham's own blends of tobacco. Percy Lovejoy became his partner in 1890 and the business continues today under the guidance of David Wheeler. At the other end of the street was another tobacconist, Abraham Crofton Rippon, who took over the business from Mrs Absell in the 1880s. He set about putting

new life into this old shop. A contemporary writer said that Rippon's knowledge 'commanded the custom of a first class clientele!' He would tell of how Ralph Lane, first governor of Virginia became the first English smoker and of how Raleigh smoked his pipe before going to the scaffold. He would tell his customers of tobacco's medicinal and soothing qualities and of how it had literary, philosophic and even religious attributes, and would quote the famous preacher Spurgeon—who was associated with Marlow Road Baptist Church—as ending an oration at the Tabernacle in 1874 with the words, 'I intend to smoke a good cigar to the glory of God before I go to bed to-night'. His lady customers, who were said to include a countess, were advised on which cigarettes best suited their nerves or physical health. Rippon died in 1915 aged 77. Snuff, such as Cardinal, the aromatic variety, held its popularity for many years. Certain trades, especially printing, contained many snuff takers. It was sold at grocers who displayed the familiar sign 'Licensed for the sale of tea, coffee, pepper, tobacco (snuff), and vinegar'.

Queen Street, when it appeared in 1872, was originally called New Road. Before Messers the timber merchants established themselves there in 1880, Smith and Johnson took the site (which was to become a timber yard) for use as a tannery, setting up pits for pickling skins at the rear. The tanner, who had the delightful name of Thomas Colombus Smith, eventually bought Ockwells Manor and built a new tannery in Ockwells Road. The old Manor was eventually rescued by Sir Edward Barry, who restored it, and set up a covenant on surrounding land to prevent future development encroaching on it.

The most influential of all High Street traders until his fall from grace, was Robert Walker. He ran the chemist's business, Higgs & Walker, a site now occupied by the Midland Bank. But in character it was closer to a general store. In 1850 it was also the Post Office and a general printing office from which he published an annual *Year Book of Useful Knowledge*. It was also a newsagent's whence Walker would let out *The Times* on contract. The well-to-do bought their lamp oil there, the poor having to be satisfied with Nicholson's rush lights and candles. Walker was also the sole agent for Dr Epp's homeopathic cocoa, while the chemist's side made up its own medicines—altogether, a comprehensive emporium.

Outside business he was a prominent Methodist and teetotaller, having laid more chapel foundation stones than any other Maidonian. He had interests also in the original gas company and later the water company. It was he who opened Maidenhead station in 1871, for which he had campaigned, and which was built by William Woodbridge. Walker was also the first to wear the red mayoral robe which he had bought and presented to the Corporation. But like other good men before and since, he became involved with a group of local politicoes, unwittingly it is thought, through his interests in the progress of the town, and this brought a disastrous end to his career in public life.

In the 1870s there was a movement to introduce piped water. Previously it had been drawn from community wells. There was a town pump at the corner of King Street and High Street. Marshall's Pump was in King Street, Wick's Pump at Dolman's Buildings. There was an Albert and Victoria Street pump, and deep wells on Castle Hill and Boyn Hill. The well-off had their own. When Silvers built Boyn Hill reservoir and the Castle Hill well was sunk for the water company—it was worked by second-hand pumps bought from Brighton Water Works—the nearby community wells were put out of action.

When the Corporation prepared its water works scheme some members were influenced by a group of company promoters for, it was thought, private gain. There was a rift among them, and the 1874 election was fought on the issue. Walker's name became linked with the company promoters. Two petitions were lodged against them, one by that upstanding local citizen, W. Nicholson. The accusations were of bribery, treating voters in the pubs, corrupt practices, and of exercising undue influences before, during, and after the election. The trial in March 1875 lasted three days. Witnesses included James Leaver of the Metal Works, a string of licensees, the printer of the election handbills, and many others. Judge C.J. Coleman ruled that some seats, including Walker's, should be declared vacant. It was a terrible blow to Walker, from which he never recovered. He retired from public affairs to live in one of his villas facing Kidwells Park. But the public did not believe that he was guilty, and when he died in 1886, aged 64, the town gave him one of those spectacular funerals that the Victorians did so well. Both teetotallers and drinkers joined in the massed march to the Wesleyan Church, with Oddfellows, Foresters and Buffaloes all wearing their regalia. These official bodies headed a throng of ordinary people, who filled both the chapel and the road outside. His son Wesley Walker carried on the business, became an alderman, and like his father, a pillar of local society.

Dignity, however, was not all that counted in High Street trading. It was certainly not the first thought of Mr Fisher who introduced rhyming advertising. Though it lacked the slick copywriting of today, it evidently helped him to move from Bridge Street up-market to No 75 High Street. He was a bootmaker.

Have you heard the latest news
About the wondrous boots and shoes?
The shop where O so many go
At Fishers, Bridge Street, Maidenhead.

There children's shoes of wondrous sight,
Big, little, stout, and light,
The quality and price all right
At Fishers, Bridge Street, Maidenhead.

At Six and nine there's women's leather,
Strong and Soundly put together
Fit to wear in any weather,
At Fisher's, Bridge Street, Maidenhead.

Side spring boots of great renown,
As good as any in the town,
From three and nine for ready brown
At Fisher's, Bridge Street, Maidenhead.

His Balmorals will make you stare
Sure ne'er such boots were made to wear
None's fame in these so widely spread
At Fisher's, Bridge Street, Maidenhead.

There's ankle shoes of all descript
With famous nails and polished tip
For working men they're just the clip
At Fisher's Bridge Street, Maidenhead.

Stout Wellingtons a pound a pair
The best in all the world to wear
They're out to fit unto a hair
At Fisher's Bridge Street, Maidenhead.

Repairing too is done so well
Your own old boots you cannot tell
And what I say I tell you true
They're often better than when new.

He pays attention to his trade
And customers of every grade
May come and have their shoes home made.

(Bundles of Balmorals and Wellingtons hung outside his shop. 'Brown' was a slang term for copper coins.)

Two High Street businesses, which eventually disappeared from the street after World War II, were so admired and respected that their interment in the archives came close to bringing the town out in public mourning. One of these was founded by James Courtis Webber, which grew from Caleb Coleman's draper's shop at No 62. Mr Webber did everything in style. It became a carriage trade establishment with workrooms for a large staff of milliners and dressmakers. The apprentices lived in and young girls wanted to work there. Its fashion parades employed professional models and drew audiences of hundreds. Eventually it also had a restaurant. Webber took over Nos 78 & 79. He was known to all as 'The Chief'. J.C. Webber was a little frock-coated figure who was to influence the modes and manners of the town for long after he died. Some of the best small businesses in town came to be run by people who had learned their trade from his business. His style of trading also carried on for some years, though he was no longer at the helm.

The other was founded by Edward Thomas Biggs. Mr Biggs opened as a watch and clockmaker on the south side of High Street, later moving across to No 32. He was also the town's first pawnbroker in the 1860s. His family carried the business on until recent years. The shop came to deal in the most exquisite merchandise and displayed one of the finest collections of Georgian silver. Queen Mary became a customer. Edward Biggs was a founder of Maidenhead Football Club in 1869 and its treasurer. He was prominent in the local art movement, vicar's warden at St Mary's, and one of the organisers and the first member of the Constitutional Club. He died in 1919 aged 77.

But the family that has probably had a greater influence upon the town than any other is the Stuchberys. Originally Buckingham brewers, they opened Stuchbery's Stores (now International), taught Nicholson to brew beer, and founded the legal firm which bears their name. Another old Maidenhead family to have disappeared from High Street since World War II is the Neves. John Neve, Mayor in 1969, was the last proprietor.

Julius came from Kent in 1847, a follower of John Calvin. He held religious meetings over his outfitter's shop in High Street and in the York Road school room. He built the York chapel in 1865, which is still there. Like other Maidonians of his day, he was a bit of a naturalist and interested in art and literature. He had an aviary of canaries, bullfinches and linnets in his shop and was one of the first supporters of the Literary Institute.

Businessmen soon demanded local banking facilities. Probably the first local bank was the Maidenhead Savings Bank which was founded in 1820 and opened on the first and third Tuesdays in every month. It was promoted by John Lewington, an estate agent, who was mayor in 1829 and borough treasurer for a number of years. But High Street banking as we know it dates from about 1837 when Stephens, Stephens, Blandy & Co opened a bank at the corner of Market Street and High Street. Treasury notes were unknown. Gold, silver and copper were the currency. Lloyds took it over and William Morris became the manager. Another manager, H.J. Mount, became the secretary of Maidenhead Building Society (now part of the London & South of England) and Worshipful Master of the Ellington Lodge of Freemasons. Masonry was fairly widespread in the town.

There were, of course, holidays from all this intensive trading. Indeed there was an annual one on Easter Monday. That was the day when the town mounted up and headed

for the meet of the Royal Buckhounds, on the Thicket at the Coach and Horses. The exodus from town crowded the winding way to the Thicket Tollgate, which was exactly one mile from the milestone at Boyn Hill passing Reading Pond, a spring at Boyn Hill, after which Pond House is named. All the trotting horseflesh and turnouts in town joined the route to the meet. Brakes, wagonettes loaded with ordinary people, dog carts, hacks, cobs, ponies, even donkeys made their noisy way westwards. Hawkers and mine host Mason did a roaring trade. It was such a regular event, that even the hounds seemed to know the royal stag and would not harrass him. Indeed one stag called Cetewayd became so well-known, that riders would draw abreast of him and pat his neck while the hounds ambled close by. The tollgate was there until 1864, when it was abolished. The Highways and Locomotive Act made turnpikes into main roads.

Brunel's railway also became involved in hunting early in 1882, when for the first time in living memory the Queen's Royal Staghounds met outside the Bear Hotel in High Street. Although it is unlikely that any Victorian shopkeeper closed his premises for the event, High Street filled with riders, pedestrians, and onlookers in open carriages. The London division of the Hunt, unaware that Maidenhead had a railway station other than Boyn Hill which was still shown in the GWR timetable, travelled to Slough by train with 30 horses and galloped over to the Bear. The hunt returned a few weeks later and a report of the event states that it was the first occasion that women were seen wearing trousers in the town. 'One or two gentlemen had put on aprons whilst as many ladies had adopted trousers. The change was not pleasant to fastidious eyes.' The deer was released at Shoppenhangers and eventually ran into the Thames where it was surrounded by hounds in the water. It was caught in a punt and taken downstream to Ray Mead Hotel where it was safely put back in the van.

But within a few years the crowds were to reverse direction and make for the river. The arrival of the railway brought this about. But once the railway had crossed the river, over Brunel's Sounding Arch, the company was pressed to build a station close to the business life of the town. At that time the only station in the town was at Boyn Hill. The bricked up entrance to it can still be seen on Castle Hill. This belonged to the Wycombe railway, which was a bit of a shoestring job. The station was little more than a hut, and the wooden viaduct across the Thames at Cookham rocked alarmingly every time a train crossed over it. Even though the town did have Mr Fry's one-horse omnibus to carry intending passengers to Taplow Station (Maidenhead, Riverside) the facilities hardly seemed appropriate for a town which believed itself to be growing in importance. So it was that Boyn Hill Station closed down when Maidenhead's opened in 1871, the GWR took over the Wycombe branch, and Mr Chamberlain's familiar call—he was the porter-station master—'Bine-ill Maidenhead', was heard no more.

As the river rather than the Thicket began to beckon holiday-makers, the slender steam launches, moored to white posts near the larger riverside properties, were soon joined by skiffs and punts and craft of all kinds, as prosperous tradesmen and their families took their fun among the growing number of visitors to the river, mingling with the Skindles' parties, and watching the wealthy at play.

FLOOD PLAIN

ABOVE: The Great Flood of 1894. The supplies go through in Bridge Road. BELOW: Ladders at the upper floors in Chummies Row, The Moor.

ABOVE: Rescue and transportation by punt. CENTRE: Bridge Road, always an early casualty. Tom Allen (left) was a cycle maker and lived in West Street. BELOW: Flood waters collapsed Moor Arch. Tom Hine saved a man who was washed under this arch.

53

ABOVE: Fence high at Ray Lodge. CENTRE: Business as usual in waders at Tom Hine's the Butcher's. BELOW: The isolated Ark in Ray Street.

ABOVE: Ray Mill Road in the Flood Plain. The river is in the distance.
(MC) CENTRE: Highways became rivers even in summer floods (1903).
(MC) BELOW: Dancing girls outside Somersham, Ray Park Avenue.

ABOVE: June, 1903 at Boulters, and BELOW: Bridge Road in 1894.

COLLECTORS' ITEMS

Whitmore & Son's Leather Works, 106 High Street—the business began about 1826—sold a navvy boot, farmer's boot, police boot, waterman's boot, school boot, and a Cookham boot.

Board of Trade Report (1845) criticised broad gauge systems and stressed the poor speeds of GWR trains, then averaging only 33 mph. Stung into action, the GWR then produced the fastest trains in the world, the locomotives endearing themselves to railwaymen and public alike. (Tony Anderson's *Farewell to Steam, Advertiser Supplement* 1969)

Five partners invested £100 between them and relied on an overdraft on a note of hand for £200 with the London and County Bank (now Natwest) to meet running costs, according to an old *Advertiser* minute book. That was how the newspaper began. A minute of 1871 reads: 'The Editor having complained of the staff being negligent and careless it was resolved that the whole staff be dismissed next quarter day'. Total wage bill at the time was £4 5s.

Private bathrooms for ladies and gentlemen at H & J Bloomfield's 2 Elm Terrace, Broadway. Hot, cold, shower, and sea water baths always ready. (Advertisement 1874)

'The police, like all our borough matters, are in a most unsatisfactory state and the sooner some improvement takes place the better', was the opinion of the *Advertiser* in 1872. In 1888 the whole force was sacked.

W. Francis, Swan Inn. Port, sherry 1s 6d; old wine 2-5s, wines from wood in half-pint bottles 8d (including bottle), brandy 4s 6d, whiskey 3s. Private sitting rooms and well-aired beds. (Advertisement 1874).

At the annual meeting of Maidenhead FC in 1877 members were told that throwing in from the side would materially alter the game. Shortly afterwards a cross bar replaced the tape on goal posts.

A drunk with a wooden leg was approached by a policeman in 1881 who sought to arrest him. He hit the constable in the face with a quarten loaf to begin with, then set about him with his wooden leg. It took the constable and Superintendent Taylor some time to tie him to a stretcher on which he was borne to the lock-up.

When the Primitive Methodist Chapel in Queen Street (now Salvation Army Citadel) opened in 1882, Mr Robert Walker ended his address with the words: 'Thank God my friends, take courage, and pay your pew rents'.

In May 1883, shop workers appealed for early closing in these terms. 'We are close by a magnificent river with every facility for enjoyment thereon, besides numerous other sports which would invigorate the soul and raise in the mind sublime ideas ... summer is now rapidly approaching with all her beauties and we are compelled to stay at business until 8 o'clock ... we don't ask for all the year round, say from May to September'. The appeal was for early closing on one night a week at 5 pm.

In 1836 the Town Clerk earned £40 per annum. In 1883, Alderman Loveridge moved: that an assistant or deputy clerk be appointed and that the Town Clerk's salary be reduced to provide a portion of the same. (Council minutes).

F.W. Simpoze, 7 Garden Cottages, The Furniture Hospital. Chairs recaned &c moths exterminated. (Advertisement, 1886)

Fire at Temple House: The pumpers who assisted Maidenhead Fire Brigade must attend at the Greyhound Hotel on Monday night next at 7.30 when they will be paid for their services. J.K. Bolton, hon sec. (Advertisement, 1886)

In 1883 there were thirty subscribers to the new telephone service. Annual subscription was eight guineas and local calls were free to subscribers. Non-subscribers paid sixpence. The manager, Mr G.W. Pike, with A.C. Hewitt, invented and patented a fire escape.

In May, 1890, Daisy Stanley, a teacher of calisthenics, led her Original Lady Cricketers on to the pitch at Maidenhead. The *Advertiser* carried a report of an interview with their manager, Mr Michel, who said it was of vast importance that the respectability of the girls should be above suspicion because they played most of their matches among the gentry. Their skirts were long and weighted with shot so that they could not lift in the wind. They wore combination undergarments made in one piece so nothing could occur to shock their modesty or that of the spectators. Across the breast they wore steel plates, leather, and wadding.

Value of stamps sold in 1891 by Maidenhead Post Office was £600,000. Some 30,000 letters and 1,000 parcels were delivered weekly. The telegraph service (Morse) began about 1872.

Much of the degeneracy of modern youth arises from the demoralising influence of football, which is a rowdy and gambling game. Saturday matches cause neglect of religious duty on Sundays. (The Rev. W.G. Sawyer, rector of Taplow, 1893)

'An amateur club is the most becoming cradle of my profession. I have watched with great interest the remarkable growth of amateur clubs ...' (Sir Henry Irving, president, Maidenhead Histrionic Club 1895).

Clayton, Isaac, hairdresser and naturalist, 4 Market St. Fernie, William Newstead, music seller and registrar of births and deaths, 88 Queen Street. (*Kelly's Directory*, 1903)

In June, 1908, E. Andrews received the following instruction from Colonel Legge, equerry to King Edward VII: 'Require your best electric launch—Angler is it not—and best man, at the King's boathouse opposite Datchet, 3.30 tomorrow (Saturday) afternoon. State how many boat accommodates and telegraph immediately'. (The best man was Joseph Tindall and the steer hand H. Matthews). The King and Queen Alexandra cruised on Monkey Island with a party of friends where they had tea on the lawn. Mr Plummer, Queen Street photographer, who happened to be there, was requested by the King to photograph the party.

ABOVE: Horton Grange, home of the Seebohm brothers opposite Boulters Lock. BELOW: Skindles with rowing types round Bond's boathouse in foreground. Oars and a weighing machine are at the entrance.

ABOVE: The beginning of cars,and horses in High Street. BELOW: St Ives Road with the cedar outside the first borough library. INSET: David MacFarlane.

ABOVE: Park Street frontage of the old Town Hall. Old police cells were in the building left. BELOW: High Street celebrates Mafeking Night in May, 1900.

ABOVE: Queen Street in 1904. BELOW: Maidenhead's most popular Postmaster Charles Cleare (left) with Jane Cleare, Henry Cleare (right) who ran the Dumbell Hotel, and Amelia Cleare.

ABOVE: Rear view of Mr Cleare's post office in High Street. BELOW.
Victorian postal staff including the telegraph boys (front row).

ABOVE: The Brigade of Guards Boat Club's premises. BELOW: An early tricycle outside the George Hotel, Bray (now Waterside). Cycle manufacturing in Maidenhead was begun by the Timberlake family in the 1860s. INSET: Norfolk Park Working Men's Club. (MC)

LEFT: *An early bicycle, with rider. (BCM) RIGHT: A Boneshaker:
identical to the first machine made by Henry Timberlake. (BCM) BELOW.
Park House, York Road where private education began in Maidenhead.*

Norfolk Park School where tradesmen's sons and daughters were educated. ABOVE: The boys in 1907, (MC) and BELOW: the junior division, 1906. (MC)

*Norfolk Park School again: with ABOVE: junior girls, 1907, (MC) and
BELOW: senior division, 1906. (MC)*

ABOVE: Norfolk Park senior girls, 1907. (MC) LEFT: Schoolboys play at four-in-hands, (MC) and RIGHT: what the well-dressed schoolboy looked like at the turn of the century. (MC)

68

ABOVE: Pioneers of the Maidenhead Adult School. BELOW: Sporting types in sporting gear.

69

ABOVE: Cricket as it was dressed for, with Alderman C.W. Cox between the two ladies in the hats. BELOW: Bowls and runner beans at the Gardeners' Arms. An early picture of women at play.

ABOVE: Bowls, watch chains and salubrious surroundings, at Maidenhead Bowling Club. Front Row: Bill Burnham, Jim Barley, Sir Ernest Gardner MP, T. Street, J. Brooks, Tom Marsh. Also in the picture are: Frank Porter, A. Sleath, Percey Lever, F. Pitcher, Frank Curtis, G. Gude, J. Mitchell, G. Grinstead. The Chairman was Captain Henry Hoare, the Treasurer W. Naylor, the Secretary J. Barley, and the annual subscription was 12s 6d. BELOW: What a well-dressed wedding party looked like. (MC)

SOCIAL PATTERNS

Gradually the new community growing around the High Street shops and the professional men began to make social patterns. From the start the Victorians were good organisers. They liked to have everything in its place and that included people. All over the country, a powerful middle class was beginning to assemble and expand around successful traders, as the country settled into one of its longest periods of peace, and the era of private trading began. Maidenhead was no exception. The borough became increasingly independent and detached from the rural area, as a long line of High Street mayors gathered about them men of business to wield their influence over civic matters. Around them the new elite began to grow. At another level, a respected and respectful artisan class extended into all departments of shopkeeping and trading and into the public services that the new borough required. The two other levels of society were both at some distance from the High Street mainstream. The upper crust, such as the Grenfells, were expected to behave as such, while the labourers and deserving poor, of whom there quite a few, were expected to serve their masters without complaint. This layer really came off worst out of the whole package. The driving power of the Victorians lay in the centre—the nation of shopkeepers—there were the entrepeneurs and the men of enterprise.

It was inevitable that the Victorians should begin by educating their families, so that they also would grow to take up positions of influence, and be able to contribute to the general progress which their parents intended. A new industrial age was beginning and the horizons were ever-extending. The Victorians were well-aware of the value of education and they began by setting up a private schools system with a leaning towards science. It was before the days of strident party political strife. Rather did the influences come from trade and the church.

J.D.M. Pearce, who was the son of a Congregational minister and one of our busiest Victorians, had designed and built Craufurd College, a young gentleman's boarding school, which opened in the 1840s. It was equipped with science laboratories. He was particularly interested in electricity and magnetism, the exploration of which was just beginning. A number of other educational establishments soon appeared. A man called Augustus John Havell bought a piece of land in York Road and built Park House on it—the present headquarters of the RWVS—where he established a private school. Another private academy, the Lyons School, was set up in Norfolk Park, the new estate to the north of High Street. Mr A. Millar Inglis, who died as recently as 1941, had opened Norfolk Park school which later moved to Ingleside in the Crescent. John Jones, who was the master of the British School in Brock Lane, eventually followed Augustus Havell at Park House, where in addition to Latin, French and music, science was taught. This school amalgamated with the Lyons School to become the nucleus from which emerged Maidenhead College, built by A. Millar Inglis in 1891, known today as the Convent. Maidenhead Commercial School Co Ltd opened the town's first secondary school in 1894, called The Modern School. The County Girls' School, now Newlands, arrived in 1905.

Education of a most elementary kind for poorer people had existed for some years with

charitable support. Funds from the 18th century Spoore, Merry and Rixman charities were used to support the National Schools in 1817, for the education of the poor in the principles of the established church. The duties of girls in Maidenhead's National Schools included knitting, making up and mending clothes, and household work. The mistress got half the profit from the girls' work as part wages. There was a buyers' market in domestic servants. Maidenhead Congregationalists started the British School in 1848; Wesleyan schools appeared in 1843, All Saints in 1857, and the Catholic schools in 1871. The British and Wesleyan schools were superseded by Gordon Road School.

There was therefore, a strong science base in the middle class schools, while the others concentrated on the skills required by artisans. But the science taught at Craufurd College could be encountered at evening classes by all who wished to attend, because Mr Pearce was intent upon spreading the knowledge and began a system of night schools. Pearce was a tremendous local worker for the benefit of the town generally. He was five times mayor and gave Kidwells Park to the town. These evening activities were soon to embrace the arts and literary subjects. There was a certain democracy in knowledge at local clubs and meeting places for all who cared to join in, though entrance fees no doubt rationed this facility to some extent.

The borough's interest in the arts was fuelled by these clubs and societies who were influenced, no doubt, by the town's long association with well-known art and literary figures of the day. The Victorian poet Thomas Noel ('Rocked in the Cradle of the Deep') lived and worked at Boyne Cottage, Boyn Hill. He was a friend of the Berkshire authoress Mary Russell Mitford, and distantly related to Lady Byron. Charles Kingsley's father married Fanny, daughter of Pascoe Grenfell of Taplow Court. His daughter, St Ledger Kingsley became a well-known novelist writing under the name of Lucas Malet. Max Muller lived at Ray Lodge for a number of years up to mid-Victorian times and it is believed that he wrote his *Science of Language* there. In 1859, he married Georgiana, sister of the wives of Charles Kingsley and J.A. Froud (1818-1894), the historian who was Carlyle's literary executor. Mortimer Collins who wrote for *The Times* lived at Knowl Hill. The brothers Seebohm—Frederick a student of history, social and political development, and Henry the ornithologist and author—lived at Horton Grange, Boulters Lock. It was formerly Sandhill Close. Henry was interested in the migration of birds and people would arrive at Horton Grange with specimens for him to inspect.

There was also native talent, particularly Zerubbabel Wyvill, organist at St Mary's and composer of hymns and other music. He lived in Pope's Lane, which led from High Street and joined with Brock Lane and South Street. His son, Robert, of 78 High Street, was also organist at St Mary's and a teacher. In 1867 he left £400 (Wyvill's Charity) 'for the distribution of bread, coal and clothing at Christmastide to the deserving poor'.

Another gifted local musician was Joseph Silver, son of Richard the builder. Joseph built organs, as later did his son-in-law J.S. Mead. Even the building firm became renowned for its beautiful churches. Among their work was a new stone ceiling in the south chapel at Dorchester Abbey. Then there were individual musicians such as William Burnham, the High Street stationer, who was occasionally summoned to Windsor Castle to play his double bass viol in Queen Victoria's orchestra. From these arty interests sprang the amateur theatre and its musical groups.

Perhaps the strongest unifying force in the town as a whole was its sporting interest. Maidenhead's cricket club records go back beyond those of the MCC. Cricket and football enjoyed enormous support from all quarters. The middle classes and the artisans joined together on the field of sport. There was also a certain primitive democracy about the social clubs, particularly the Norfolk Park Working Men's Club. The upper crusters and the professional men were brought into this social arena as presidents, patrons, and philanthropists. The Norfolk Park club was founded by Pearce and Robert Sawyer, another ardent temperance worker.

The president of the first art class was Dr Plane, whose surgery was just below the Midland Bank in High Street, formerly Colebrooks. He came here from the Crimea about 1859, to be joined later by Dr Goolden of the Wilderness, Dr Moore, and Dr Mason who took the name Mason-Macfarlane. His son was Major-General Mason Macfarlane. Dr Plane helped to found Maidenhead Cottage Hospital: the foundation stone was laid in 1879. Another of his interests was archaeology, a popular Victorian pursuit. Mr Millar Inglis, outside school, played both cricket and football for Maidenhead. Another footballer, Alderman E.W. Mackie, mayor 1875-76, (he played outside left) was credited with cleaning up the municipal mess of the period and generally regarded by Victorians, with Richard Silver the builder, and William Nicholson the brewer, as a man whose record of service to the town would be hard to beat.

There was a further overlapping of interests in the annual event known as the Industrial Exhibition, which was held at Norfolk Park WMC. This club evolved into the Conservative Working Men's Club, currently in York Road. At one of these exhibitions both masters' and artisans' work was described in an *Advertiser* report. Exhibits included John Kinghorn Cooper's fine terra cotta work, Miss L. Cooper's oil painting, a case of brass cannon by Alec Norvall of Leaver's Metal Works, sign writing by Joe Rust, an exhibition of mechanical dentistry by Alfred Starling ('We thought it the last word in the production of artificial teeth'), exhibition bicycle riding on a penny farthing by W.T. Dobson of the Wanderers' Bicycle Club, a plaster work display by W.J. Gilroy. W. Blowfield of West Street showed specimen horse shoes, and W.K. Harper, club steward, a collection of butterflies, all caught within the borough. But the most interesting exhibit, perhaps showing the influence of Mr Pearce's school through its interests in new technology, was a Cabinet of Electricity, illustrating, according to the *Advertiser*, 'the various uses to which this wonderful assest in nature are now applied'. Afterwards it stood in the showrooms of George Farmiloe & Son, in St John's Street, London, and brought much electrical work to Maidenhead.

Thus, doctors, dentists, teachers, councillors and craftsmen, joined into groups as footballers, painters, musicians or archaeologists, and those with a public conscience came forward to do voluntary work of one kind or another. The new Cottage Hospital became a magnet for much of this. An enormous amount of Maidenhead effort from all levels of society went into the running of this hospital, which was demolished in 1979.

For the more adventurous there was the volunteer fire brigade. Although a brigade was in existence prior to 1866, run under the auspices of the Watch Committee, a town fire brigade, properly dressed, did not begin until the following year, when handbills were distributed to invite subscriptions. Prominent citizens, such as William Nicholson

organised the collections in various districts. It was in that year that the Fire Brigade Committee called upon local shopkeepers to tender for helmets, tunics and belts. Curiously there was no mention of trousers. Among those who tendered was Alfred Cull, the hatter of High Street. His business was next door to the old Swan. The successor of this business is still going today. When Alfred Cull retired to Guernsey, the business was managed by T.G. Wyatt and Tom de la Hay. Eventually it divided into two separate businesses. T.G. Wyatt joined Alderman Good to form Good & Wyatt and R.G. Bott later bought it. It continues today in the Shopping Precinct. Like everybody in town who was anybody, Alfred Cull belonged to the Rifle Volunteers; he had a tenor voice and sang at local concerts, being yet another High Street man who became involved in the town's social life. The successful tender for tunic, belt and helmet was for £1 10s.

MAIDENHEAD VOLUNTEERS

Again and again shall the humorous Muse,
 Diffuse information and help to amuse,
And what better theme can she bring from her store
 Than the famous "Fifth Berkshire Rifle Corps."

Comparisons are very odious we know,
 And those who're eclipsed will surely think so,
But for soldierly qualities none stand before,
 This very renowned "Berkshire Rifle Corps."

For the gallant and brave, and the wise and the great,
 The eloquent, musical, light and sedate,
With those who the cannon have braved at death's door,
 United are found in this "Fifth Rifle Corps."

There's Captain Vansittart of wonderful fame,
 Lieutenant E. Sawyer, and Ensign Micklem,
While Grenfell for quartering all the world o'er,
 Is the man of all others for this "Rifle Corps."

Sergeant Major is Smith, and the next men of mark,
 Sergeants Durrant and Cull, Edward Shayler and Clark,
Then Fuller, Sykes, Jackson and Poulton are four,
 Who as Corporals rank in this "Rifle Corps."

A position of pride was attained on the day
 When "All Berkshire" competed in splendid array,
For the Challenge Cup prizes; but the contest so sore,
 Was decided in favour of this "Rifle Corps."

Nearly 90 of all sorts and sizes we see,
 Who volunteer thus in the field to agree,
And if need be to fight 'midst the cannon's roar,
 Hurrah, for the "Fifth Berkshire Rifle Corps."

Prevention is better than cure we well know,
 So Britain is arming in case of a foe,
The only one likely lives close at our door,
 'Tis France has created all our "Rifle Corps."

Volunteers; Volunteers; we greet you with joy,
 In peace may you live and in peace may you die,
May the enemy never on England's shore,
 Contend with the "Fifth Berkshire Corps."

But if this event should awaken our fears,
 Or the news of his landing should trouble our ears,
With God's blessing we hope he will soon fall before
 Our "United Volunteer Rifle Corps."

In those days the horses were stabled at the Saracen's Head and the keys to the engine house were kept at the Post Office, then adjoining Red Lion Square. The alarm was sounded on the bells of St Mary's and the Wesleyan Churches. The regulations stated that in cases of fire, the secretary was to be informed immediately along with members of the brigade, and a notice posted outside the Town Hall. Bureaucracy had evidently begun. No mention is made of whether the bellringers could start their peals without the authorisation of the secretary, but there was no mistaking the dash and urgency which the members brought to their turnouts. The fire engine, a manual affair, would roar out of the Saracen's Head yard at breakneck speed with 'General' Jackson in charge. He was a butcher of Lower High Street. This was close to the time when General Stonewall Jackson fought the battle of Bull Run and earned a reputation for staying power—hence the nickname. General Jackson stayed for a long time. He was a children's hero for three

decades. They would leave their marbles, rounders, and other games to crowd into Durrant's Meadow (York Road Football Ground) to watch him and the brigade at fire practice. Jackson himself fitted the pattern of High Street traders exactly. He sang at Penny Readings in the old town hall in the '70s, and with members of his brigade, belonged to the dramatic society and helped raise brigade funds through entertaining. This was how the original Maidenhead institutions were created and built—by the town working for them. He retired in 1891. The public subscribed a purse of £150 10s for him. He died the following year, to be given the biggest funeral the town had ever seen. Early records show that the first fire attended by the uniformed brigade was a rick at Pond House, Waltham, on November 6, 1867; the second was at Boveney Court, and the third and fourth were rick fires at Bray Farm. Industrial relations, apparently, were not too good then, with the management being blamed. It was reported that 'The efforts of the brigade were seriously retarded by the refusal to work of the labouring men because they had not been paid by the fire office for their efforts at the previous fire'. There is a nice distinction here between volunteers and labourers. The first serious fire in town was in the newly-built tower of All Saints' Church on June 27, 1868. The bells melted.

In 1876 Joseph Henry Clark presented the brigade with 'a sort of gas mask with eye glasses and a respirator for rescue work'. One of his sons, Harry, became a fireman and aferwards a professional fire chief in America. But the fire brigade had its off-periods. After a High Street fire in 1903, the *Advertiser* carried a letter which read 'The volunteer fire brigade has added one more to its long list of displays of inefficiency. That Shand and Mason steamer seems a long time coming and the hose appears sadly defective.' After Sir Roger Palmer's death, Lady Palmer presented the town with its first motor fire engine (£1,100) which was christened *Sir Roger*.

Maidenhead in 1866 had a population of only 5,034. In 1911 it was 15,218. In those 45 years the Victorians built a thriving small town and began most of the institutions we have today. Their families have disapproved of change ever since. In 1869 J.H. Clark and a group of local businessmen founded the *Maidenhead Advertiser*. It made a rocky start and was shortly taken over by Frederick George Baylis, whose family has run it from that time. Frederick Baylis was one of those who helped to set up the Cottage Hospital. It was a report in his newspaper of a man injured while tunnelling for chalk in Louche's Chalk Pit (we call it Grenfell Park) that helped to rouse public opinion. FGB campaigned for a hospital and an early supporter was John Hibbert of Braywick Lodge.

There was also a lighter side to local affairs, especially along the riverside. The idea of Thames-side as a playground was beginning, and a number of ladies were said to have set a fashion for what became quite common in later years along the river. It was called Bohemianism. As late as 1917 the Bear Hotel sharply excluded itself from any connection with such goings-on by advertising 'No Bohemianism'. One of the ladies was Mrs Ballantine of Ray Park Avenue. She would receive workmen and others while lying in bed. An *Advertiser* account also mentions Mrs Anstruther and her daughter who 'also came under notice for their love of negligee and scanty attire'. People noticed these things in a small community. Mrs Ballantine was married to one of the most distinguished advocates of the day. Sergeant Ballantine was one of the last eight sargeants-at-law and appeared in the Sir Roger Tichbourne trial (1871-1872).

*ABOVE: Coronation day in High Street, 1911 and BELOW: a fashionable
crowd at Maidenhead Regatta.*

LEFT: Houseboats were popular in sleepy summer days. RIGHT: Queueing for Boulters and BELOW: Boulters on Whit Monday, 1901. (MC)

ABOVE: Steam launches at Boulter's tail over-looked by Glen Island.
BELOW: Advertising a Town Hall show in the Station Yard. In the
background is the office of the short-lived Maidenhead Chronicle.

Smart turn-outs for high steppers.

80

ABOVE: Gurney's High Street establishment. They were sheet metal workers and braziers. BELOW: When butchers displayed their wares. This is R.E. Plevey.

81

ABOVE: A bear being led along Norfolk Road. Performing bears, and the cruel sport of bear-baiting with dogs which once flourished in Berkshire, disappeared with the new century. BELOW: Diamond Jubilee Celebrations, in High Street. Centre left is the Falcon Inn. Barclays Bank was built there.

*ABOVE: Return of local volunteers from South Africa. BELOW:
Proclamation of the death of Victoria on the steps of the Town Hall.*

Diamond Jubilee celebrations in Grenfell Park, the former Chalk Pit given to the town by William Grenfell (Lord Desborough) two years later in 1899.

*ABOVE: Beating the bounds of the borough has taken place periodically.
In 1886 Mayor William Woodbridge, who built a great deal of Maidenhead
led the party. BELOW: The perambulators in 1889.*

ABOVE: An apparently small party of perambulators in 1909, but two faces are familiar, Alderman C.W. Cox, the town cryer, seated on the right, and in the second row the mace bearer, Mark Taylor. CENTRE: A traditional refreshment stop at the Thatched Cottage Public House which is almost on the boundary line. BELOW: Castle Hill before the motor car.

Daniel Herbert Brown, his wife Clara (nee Such) (left) parents of John Brown, borough and county councillor and Chelsea Show judge. The family came to Braywick in 1824, later set up Brown & Such's renowned dahlia nursery. Frederick Parker Such opened Such's Academy for poor boys at 45 Bridge Road in 1824. The family history is traceable to French royalty through Eleonore Le Sauteur, wife of Eric Frederick , great-grandfather of John Brown. (JB) INSET LEFT: Eric Frederick Such, (JB) and RIGHT: Eleonore Ann Le Sauteur. (JB)

EFT: Official opening of the Clock Tower to celebrate the Diamond ibilee. ABOVE: Maidenhead celebrates outside old Guildhall. RIGHT: Volunteer Drill Records.

VOLUNTEER'S DRILL RECORD.

Corporal J. Partlo, of the Maidenhead Company, Berks Volunteers, probably holds the record among Volunteers for regular attendance at drill. Distributing the prizes on Friday night, Mr. Ernest Gardner, M.P., congratulated Corporal Partlo on not having missed a single drill for sixteen years.

ABOVE: Volunteer Fire Brigade of 1892. In picture are: Capt Wilton, Deputy Capt Durrant, Lieut Tubb, Lieut Barford, Sub-Lieut J. Burnham, Sub-Lieut Radbourne, Pioneers, West, Hetnes, Jackson, Phillips, Whitmore, S. Lamb, T. Durrant, E. Hewitt, H. Gibson, Preece, Hewes, A. Lamb, F. Blowfield, W. Tubb, Watson, E. Butler, H. Shrimpton, Engineer Stevens, Hon drill instructor J.H. Alliston, hon sec J.K. Bolton, and two unknown schoolboys. BELOW: The brigade off duty in 1886.

ABOVE: LEFT: Brigade motorised and ready to go. (MC) RIGHT: Fire at Gude's the photographers, 7 High Street. (MC) BELOW LEFT: Back from the Boer War. RIGHT: Colonel O.P. Serocold, OC Maidenhead (G) Co, 1st Volunteer Bn, Royal Berks, 1893.

1st Vol. Batt. Royal Berkshire Regiment.

MAIDENHEAD (G) COMPANY.

July 21st, 1893.

Camp Orders for 1893.

1.—The Battalion will encamp on Farnborough Common (Camping Ground No. xix. 3) 5th to 12th August. Companies will leave Reading for North Camp, S.E.R., on 5th August, as follows: G and K Companies at 1.25 p.m.

2.—The Company will parade in marching order—undress jackets, helmets, leggings, and the whole of the new equipment, on Saturday, August 5th, and proceed to Aldershot. The hour of parade will be at 12 o'clock.

3.—One Corporal and four men, already detailed, will parade at the Armoury at 7 a.m. on Thursday, 3rd August, and proceed to Aldershot by the 7-19 a.m. train *via* Reading (reporting themselves to the Adjutant immediately on arrival) for tent pitching.

4.—The heavy baggage for camp must be at the Railway Station by 7 a.m. on Saturday, 5th August, properly labelled with name and Company. Labels can be obtained on application at the Armoury.

5.—The Baggage Party will parade at the Armoury at 7-30 a.m. on Saturday, August 5th, and proceed to Reading by the 8-3 a.m. train from Maidenhead, under the command of Col.-Sergt. Burnham.

6.—The Battalion will parade for inspection on Friday, August 11th, in Review Order. Any Officer or Volunteer absent without leave from the Inspection cannot be returned as efficient for the current year. The Camp will be broken up on the 12th August. Officers commanding companies are requested to impress upon their men the absolute necessity of their being present at the Annual Inspection of the Battalion, on Friday, August 11th. Captains of Companies will only grant leave from Inspection in cases of sickness duly certified by a medical officer; all other applications for leave are to be referred by them to the Commanding Officer through the Adjutant.

7.—Members not going to Camp are requested to send their kit bags to the Armoury, for re-issue to those members that are going.

8.—All members going to Camp are requested to carry in their haversacks the following articles, viz., pair boots, shirt, pair socks, Glengarry cap, brush and comb, towel, soap, clasp knife and lanyard, grease pot and boot laces.

9.—Members going to Camp are requested to pay their Camp Club Subscription, 10/-, to the Sergeant-Instructor on or before Saturday, 29th July, at the Armoury. No Subscriptions will be taken after that date.

10.—Letters are to be addressed in full, showing Regiment and Brigade, to Swan Inn Plateau, Aldershot.

By order,

O. P. SEROCOLD,

Captain.

Camp Orders 1893.

IMPERIAL YEOMANRY.	PRIVATE F. HUMFREY	PRIVATE T. ALLAM
LIEUTENANT A.C. PALLANT	'' A.J. GILROY	'' H.W. BLACKWELL
'' T. HAIG	'' A.G. GROVES [DIED OF DISEASE]	'' A. CAMPEY
LIEUT & QMR N.P. SNOWDEN	'' W.R. NICHOLSON	'' R. GROVES [DIED OF DISEAS
'' '' J. BLOCKLEY	'' W. SEXTON	'' C. HARRIS
Q.M. SERGT K.S. GARDNER	'' A. SMITH	'' G. LEE [KILLED IN ACTION]
FAR. SERGT A.E. NEEVE	'' W. COLLIASS	'' E.R. LITTLETON
'' '' O. BEESON	'' H.F. HUMPHREYS	'' C. MAYNARD
'' '' F.E. RACKSTRAW	'' J. SAUNDERS	'' F.W. MOORE
SERCEANT F.W. HARMER	'' T.E. BOWMAN	'' W. PLATFORD
'' E. SABLE	'' B.E. MEADE	'' W.H. ROLES
CORPORAL A. LYNN [DIED OF DISEASE]	'' H.S. WEBBER	'' W. CROSBY
'' F.S. BAMPTON	ORPS OF LECTRICAL NGINEERS.	'' H. SIMMONDS
'' C.F. BAILEY	CAPTAIN J.E. PEARCE	'' F. WEST
'' G. BOND	OYAL ERKS ECT.	'' A. COOM
'' C. RUSSELL	LIEUTENANT W.P. ALLEYNE	OMPOSITE YCLE ORPS.
'' C. DURRANT	CORPORAL A.J. TAYLOR	PRIVATE H.H. MOORE
LCE CORPL A.E. ALDRIDGE	LCE CORPL H. LITTLETON	'' T.R. NASH
PRIVATE C.B. DARBY	'' '' E.J. WOOD	
'' F.H. RUSSEL	'' '' T. MAGUIRE	

ABOVE: Soldiers of the Queen in the Royal Berkshire Regiment.
CENTRE: The Corporals' Mess. BELOW: The names of those who served
in the Boer War, (1899-1902).

Chorus Allegro Con Spirito.

O that men, would therefore praise the Lord for his goodness would therefore praise the

O that men, would therefore praise the Lord for his goodness

O that men, for his goodness would therefore praise the

O that men, for his goodness

Lord for his goodness, O that men, O that men, would therefore praise the Lord, would

for his goodness, O that men, O that men, would therefore praise the Lord, would

---

MAIDENHEAD AMATEUR HISTRIONIC CLUB.   5

Followed by a New and Original Drama in Four Acts, written
for the occasion by Mr. R. B. CALTON, entitled—

HOME AND ABROAD.

DRAMATIS PERSONÆ.

Matthew Matchlock	...	...	...	Mr. E. H. BREE.
Harry Matchlock	...	...	...	Mr. H. W. M. DANVERS.
Belverton...	...	...	...	... Mr. R. B. CALTON.
Dick Riggle	...	...	...	... Mr. H. CLARK.
Jim Sparks	...	...	...	...Mr. T. A. DURRANT.
Bessie Dornton	...	...	...	... Miss TEMPLETON.
First Sailor	...	...	...	... Mr. TOMS.
Second Sailor	...	...	...	Mr. WILLIAMS.
First Robber	...	...	...	Mr. AUGUSTUS.
Second Robber	...	...	...	Mr. W. CLARK.

Seamen, Villagers, Chorus, &c.
The new and appropriate Scenery by Mr. H. W. M. Danvers.

---

*ABOVE: Zerubbabel Wyvill was organist at St Mary's and a composer of
some merit. BELOW: A cast list taken from the book of the Maidenhead
Amateur Histrionic Club.*

The Household Brigade Steeplechases

Will take place at

HAWTHORN HILL

(Between Bracknell & Maidenhead),

ON FRIDAY AND SATURDAY,
April 10th and 11th,

UNDER NATIONAL HUNT RULES.

———

SECOND DAY.

The following race closes by 10 p.m. on TUESDAY NEXT, MARCH 17TH, to A. R. TROTTER, ESQ., 2nd Life Guards, Cavalry Barracks, Windsor.

THE FARMERS' STEEPLECHASE of 40 sov. to the winner, 10 sov. to the second, and 5 sov. to the third (given by the Household Brigade Racing Club); entrance, free; for horses the property on and since January 1st, 1896, of bonâ-fide Farmers either at present occupying, or who have occupied, since January 1st, 1895, land over which the Household Brigade Draghounds, Mr. Garth's Foxhounds, or the Berks and Bucks Farmers' Harriers hunt; four-years-old 11st., five 12st., six and aged 12st. 7lb.; a winner in 1895 or 1896 of any steeplechase to carry 7lb., of two steeplechases 14lb. extra; maiden five-years-old and upwards allowed 7lb.; professional riders 7lb. extra; ten entries, or the race may be void; about two miles and a half.

Colours must be sent with entry.

Clerks of the Course and Stakeholders, MESSRS. PRATT & CO., 9, George Street, Hanover Square, London, W.

Advertisement for the Household Brigade Steeplechases.

TEMPERANCE, BEER AND BIBLE

Until fairly recent times, beer, when it was free, and the Bible were two things which would fill the old town hall, the biggest crowd attending the annual meeting of the British and Foreign Bible Society. But each side had diplomatic representation to the other. Victorians were churchgoers and Sunday school attenders almost to a man or child. The middle classes with pianos and banjos in their drawing rooms, went to church with the rest on Sunday, if only for appearances. The upper classes accepted the duty. Sir Roger Palmer of Glen Island went by steam launch to either Cookham or Bray. But there was a smell of malting barley hanging over the town from its several breweries. The Salvation Army quartered in The Barracks—the local company had been recruited from our own temperance movement—was on permanent alert among those who had sorrows to drown, of whom there were more than a few, while Mr Ellis, the tailor of Park Street, assembled a choir in his home, there to sing Moody and Sanky hymns. They were the days upon which we now look back with nostalgic pride, as we take from a dusty case on the mantelshelf that old pair of rose-tinted spectacles and complain of the mess that the functional 20th century has made of the place, conveniently overlooking the fact that there was great poverty, a serious need for temperance, and a requirement to bring the community to a disciplined way of life. The topic of the day, in mid-Victorian times, believe it or not, was overpopulation, and there was encouragement to emigrate to the Empire, as many Maidonians did.

There were two kinds of poor, the beggars and idlers, and the 'deserving' poor. Daniel Sexton, who was appointed mayor's constable in 1836, was instructed to apprehend anyone found begging or otherwise idle, and to attend the closing of beer houses and pubs. His constables received 2s 6d per arrest. His successor, Flannel Foot Austin, chief constable in the '70s, was still keeping his eye on the undeserving poor. For the deserving, Nicholson's Brewery opened a soup kitchen every winter. The poor lined up with jugs and vessels of all kinds to scoop the soup from the beer vat. Children climbed in to lick the sides when the supply ran out. Those were not the good old days for the poor. Winter relief was a regular event. Churchmen, particularly the Methodists and Congregationalists, played a stalwart role in bringing to Maidenhead a sense of civic responsibility. Total abstainers and non-smokers such as J.D.M. Pearce, Robert Walker and William Woodbridge made enormous contributions to the growing town, pressurising it towards a strict code of morality. Pearce, whose Craufurd College was to produce a number of distinguished engineers for the new age of electricity, including his son, J.E. Pearce, was active in carrying the gospel of clean living into town life. Latimer Clark, who invented the standard cell for the measurement of electromotive force and compiled the first work on electrical measurement, was educated there. He founded the pioneer electrical firm of Clark Muirhead & Co. The college also taught instrumental band music. Bands were to be found at the head of all the town parades, not forgetting those of the temperance movement. Progressing about the streets in this manner was fairly common on public occasions.

With Robert Sawyer, another ardent temperance worker, Edward Patterson founded

the Norfolk Park Working Men's Club. The present British Legion Club in Bridge Road was also built by Pearce, as a model lodging house, because there was so much degradation at the Old Crown Lodging House, but it was not popular with the drunks. Pearce died in 1898 aged 79. The London Necropolis Company, who provided his coffin, described it thus 'non repulsive in appearance like ordinary coffins, is particularly suited to the process of natural interment facilitating the free resolvent action of the earth upon human remains'.

Others in the temperance movement were much noisier. One of these was Captain Thomas of 29 Park Street. His was an honorary rank. He had just retired from the Army and was of military bearing. An ardent Salvationist, he began a number of religious movements. In particular, he led a body of evangelical total abstainers, who wore a blue patch in their buttonholes when parading, which they often did in a provocative manner, singing their marching song. He called them The Blue Ribbon Army. Brewers and pub keepers formed a Yellow Ribbon Army, which usually marched at the same time. There were many processions and many noisy clashes. By March, 1883, local people had had enough of this rivalry and asked local magistrates to suppress the processions. They said they produced intolerable disturbances almost amounting to riots. At this time Captain Dalley was leading The Blue Ribbon Army and he appealed to the bench for protection. But the bench was not sympathetic. They told him to parade on the Moor or stay in his chapel, as information had been laid against him for obstruction. There was little temperance about his next move. Ignoring the direction from the bench, he led The Blue Ribbon Army out on to the street and into what was described as the Battle of Chapel Arches, where The Yellow Ribboners were waiting. Drums and brass instruments were smashed in the ensuing riot. The instruments had been hired from the Temperance Band for £1. The band claimed that the conditions of the hiring agreement had been broken—that they should not be exposed to damage—and withdrew them. That silenced The Blue Ribboners.

The temperance bands became well-known and were the forerunners of the Maidenhead Town Band. One of Pearce's sons, Dr Walter Pearce, house surgeon at St Mary's Hospital, founded the first Drum and Fife Band which won prizes at Crystal Palace competitions. It played for the Duke of Westminster whose country seat was Cliveden. Corporal Pearson of the Coldstream Guards became instructor for the temperance bands. Even the Rechabites had a band.

The most important woman in the temperance movement was Mrs Annie Young of Park Villas, King Street. She did much good work when it was most needed. She founded the Band of Hope and the Maidenhead Temperance Football Club. Perhaps something like the Victorians' reaction to drunkenness is needed today to combat vandalism. There were others who were total fanatics. One was Mrs Massingham who bought the Shoulder of Mutton, took it out of circulation, and lived there herself until about 1897.

Craufurd Pearce, one of the sons of the headmaster, could be said to have died of purity. He believed that he could and would conquer all the desires of the flesh and the devil by a life of strict discipline and abstention. It ruined his physical condition, and was thought to have brought about his early demise. Many prominent people supported the cause of puritanism. Robert Walker founded the Abstemious Press Forward Movement

and supported American imports such as the Juvenile Templars and the Order of Good Templars. The Band of Hope and the Ancient Order of Rechabites all had close links with the free churches. They made up a body of opinion which sought to influence more than the drinking of alcohol.

When the town petitioned for a Sunday post delivery they met heavy opposition from The Blue Ribbon Army and the puritan factions. The puritans held a meeting in the Town Hall and conveyed their opposition to the Postmaster General. They also wanted to close the pubs on Sundays. But there was a counter petition headed by Sir Roger Palmer, Charles C. Ricardo, Earl Cowley, and C. Seymour Grenfell. Sir Roger, who took part in the Charge of the Light Brigade at Balaclava, seemed unlikely to be out generalled by Captain Thomas of The Blue Ribbon Army. Before the Charge of the 600, Earl Cardigan, colonel of the 11th Hussars, said to the young Roger Palmer—he had joined the Hussars in 1853 at 21—'Here goes the last of the Cardigans'. Roger had replied 'And here goes £10,000 a year'. Both survived. Palmer was also present at the battles of Alma, Inkerman, and at the seige of Sebastopol, and by 1869 was a colonel of the Life Guards. An old Etonian, he had estates in Ireland, but he made his home at Glen Island. The Blue Ribbon Army lost the engagement.

What drink problems the town had in the 1890s were not helped by the never ending procession of tramps of both sexes towards the Cookham Union Workhouse. There were about 11,000 annually. It was a major scandal. Many of them hit the bottle on the way, and were picked up by the police in the gutter, in shop doorways, and particularly on Castle Hill, significantly perhaps, just short of the Workhouse and close to a number of pubs. They were wheeled off to the cells strapped to stretchers mounted on pram wheels.

Some pubs disappeared as the High Street developed. The Town Hall was built over the Fighting Cocks, and Barclays Bank over the Quart Pot, formerly the Falcon. Progress in later years removed a number of King Street houses, which once served the thirsty smiths of Leaver's ironworks. Originally the Cauliflower Inn in King Street stood by the Braywick Road Gate. It was known as the Poor Man's Rose. The Rose Hotel is its successor.

Of the breweries, Langton's was here in the early 17th century and supplied beer and hot cross buns on Good Friday for the schoolchildren of West Street. The Langtons provided several early mayors and John Langton's signature appears on a Corporation document of 1600. There were occasional legitimate police raids which had nothing to do with puritanism. One such was at a banquet given by the Berkshire Brewery in Keys Lane. It had been founded by George Braxton, cooper at Nicholson's. It was later known as Keys Brewery with an off licence in King Street. Nicholsons bought it. In 1862 Nicholsons employed 14 hands. By 1936 they had 150. But there were soft drinks too in King Street where W. Tilbury, landlord of the Bell Hotel opened a mineral water factory.

Pearce's grandest contribution to temperance was the building of the Cliveden Restaurant in Queen Street, in co-operation with others. It was a really well-equipped club, until it was destroyed by fire in 1919. When rebuilt it became Brocks, a fashionable coffee house, which in recent years was rebuilt as shops and offices. Nicholson's Brewery, like the Fighting Cocks and the Quart Pot, is now obliterated. The Precinct stands on the site. Part of Langton's Brewery at the corner of West Street and Market Street is about to be demolished to make way for new development.

One other battleground of the demon drink is also obliterated today—the railway station refreshment room. It took eight applications to the bench before the licence was granted. It was opposed by the Great Western Railway Abstinence Society, the Bell Hotel, the clergy, and the temperance movement. T.K. Shrimpton, licensee of the Bell, said that if the licence was granted he would lose the greater part of his trade which he estimated at between £200 and £300 a year. But the station master, H. Manger said there were 21 down and 20 up trains stopping daily for periods ranging from three minutes to more than an hour, and that 379,000 people used the station in a year.

The Hon A. Lyttleton, for the appellants, gave an undertaking that provision would be made for 3rd class passengers, in accordance with the wishes of the bench, to have a separate place with a lower tariff. Obviously the magisterial classes did not wish to be seen drinking with the lower orders. The bench approved the licence in August, 1883.

It may be that the social problem of alcohol and poverty had an association and that the puritans pursued the wrong solution. When they called a meeting at the Town Hall to stop Sunday drinking it was substantially interrupted. The *Advertiser* reported that every social club and Saturday harmonic class had practised for weeks and there was no lack of volunteers to oblige with a popular melody once the meeting opened. J.D.M. Pearce commented: 'It was the grossest violation of the right of free speech and liberty of discussion which has, in the memory of man, disgraced the town of Maidenhead'.

In 1897 women temperance workers called for a halt to children being sent to the pubs for jugs of beer. 'It led to sipping and quiet tippling by these messengers.' In 1897 the council received an account for 65 pots of beer which had been consumed by a nurse and her husband while on duty at the Isolation Hospital. Victorian thrift prompted Councillor Truscott to remark that it would have been cheaper to have sent a cask in.

Poverty was as ubiquitous as alcohol. There were regular meetings of the local Relief Committee and plenty of customers. At one of these meetings in 1892 there was 'an inrush of the ill clad and hungry including many young mothers'. Women and children were crushed against the door posts as they poured in and there was a queue outside after the hall had filled. They were seeking soup and free coal.

In 1897 Caleb Young, Walter Smith, and Robert Wilson were jailed after the anti-vaccination riots in Maidenhead. On their return from jail two thousand met them with the inevitable band. Their action led to an end to compulsory vaccination for children here. For a different reason several thousand Maidonians stormed the home of Mayor Henry Hodgson Durrant in 1887, smashing his fences and windows. They marched up the High Street from the Town Hall where they had just heard that he had been unseated as mayor. The cause of their anger was his refusal to give up part of his garden at Marlow Road Corner for road widening.

We have now widened that road, and largely cured the poverty experienced by the Victorians; the Temperance societies are less active, and even Methodists are allowed to tipple in moderation. But we finally lost the Sunday post, the private High Street trader, the convenience of local artisans and locally applied skills, trade deliveries and the presumption that the customer is always right. But we are still raising our hats to the ladies, which would please Alfred Cull.

ABOVE: The Thames Hotel before Ray Mead Road was built up. LEFT: The old St Mary's Church and Vicarage. RIGHT: The Cross Keys, last of Maidenhead's Common Lodging Houses. It opened in 1892 and closed in 1958. Its longest resident was George Lambert, who stayed for 30 years. BELOW: The pre-motoring Golden Harp at Furze Platt.

ABOVE: Harvest Festival at Waldeck (1905). (MC) CENTRE: The Cauliflower Inn (The Poor Man's Rose). It continues as the Rose Hotel, King Street. This drawing also shows the Braywick Road gate (near bottom of High Town Road). Licensee's name was R. Thatcher. LEFT and RIGHT: A token from Cliveden Temperance Restaurant and Club, Queen Street. (PR)

RESOLUTIONS

OF A

MEETING

FOR PROMOTING A DUE OBSERVANCE OF THE

Sabbath.

AT a GENERAL MEETING of the County Magistrates, Mayor, Recorder, and principal Inhabitants of the Town and Neighbourhood of MAIDENHEAD, held at the TOWN-HALL, on TUESDAY, the 17th of MAY, 1808, to consider of the best Means of promoting a due Observance of the SABBATH;

Richard Lovegrove, Esq. Mayor, in the Chair;

RESOLVED,

That the exercise of any Worldly Calling on the Lord's Day, is a direct violation of the Laws of God and Man, (except Works of Necessity and Charity.)

That to check the growing Contempt of the Sabbath, the Persons present do pledge themselves to prevent and to discountenance, to the utmost of their power, the exposing to Sale on this Day any Goods, the delivery of any Parcels by Carriers or Stage Coachmen, or other Persons employed by them, and the remaining in and Tippling in Public Houses on the Lord's Day.

That this Meeting do recommend to the several Persons employing Labourers, or other Workmen, by the Week, to pay them their Wages on the FRIDAY in each Week, in order to remove every pretence for purchasing the Necessaries of Life on the Sabbath.

That the Magistrates be requested to direct the Constables to take care that all Shops be shut during the WHOLE of the Sabbath Day; and that the Publicans do not suffer the remaining in and Tippling in Public Houses on the Lord's Day.

That the following Persons be a Committee, to act as occasion may require, in aid of the purposes of this Meeting, and to enforce the same.

The MAGISTRATES acting for the Maidenhead Division,
The MAYOR, RECORDER, BURGESSES and TOWN CLERK of Maidenhead,

The Hon. Thomas Windsor.	Rev. Edward Townshend,	Rev. John Cooke,
Sir William Herne,	Rev. Thomas Whately,	Mr. Samuel Davis,
John Sawyer, Esq.	Rev. Henry Dodwell,	Mr. William Cooper,
Lieutenant-Colonel Kearney,	Rev. William Vansittart	Mr. Joseph Poulton,
Wm, Augustus Skynner, Esq.	Rev. James Knollis,	Mr. Stephen Westbrook.

That these Resolutions be signed by the Persons present, and such others as may approve them, and be inserted once in the Reading Mercury.

That the Thanks of the Meeting be given to the Mayor, for proposing the above Resolutions, and for his Conduct in the Chair.

Richard Lovegrove, Mayor,	J. Weyland, jun.	Jos. Williams,
James Payn, Recorder,	Wm. Vansittart,	John Hussey,
J. Sawyer,	James Knollis,	Wm. Cooper,
Wm. Aug. Skynner,	Henry Dodwell,	Jos. Poulton,
Thos. Windsor,	John Langton,	Richard Swallow,
E. Townshend,	C. S. Ward, Town Clerk,	Stephen Westbrook,
Thos. Whately,	Sam. Davis,	Wm. Spurrett.
C. Hayes,	Henry Newell,	

LEFT: Poster outlining resolutions to promote 'due observance of the Sabbath'. ABOVE: Brocks' Cafe replaced the Cliveden Temperance Hotel in Queen Street after a fire. An extremely popular place it was nicknamed The Parrot House because of the women chattering there. BELOW: The Sun Inn at the foot of Castle Hill became the surgery of Doctors Maconochie, Cadogan, Flew and Pallot. OPPOSITE ABOVE: Langton's Folly, built by a member of the brewery family behind their East Street premises. BELOW: Langton's Brewery was at the corner of High Street and Marlow Road and was demolished for street improvements in 1904.

The Two Brewers stood at the corner of High Street and Marlow Road and was demolished for street improvements in 1904.

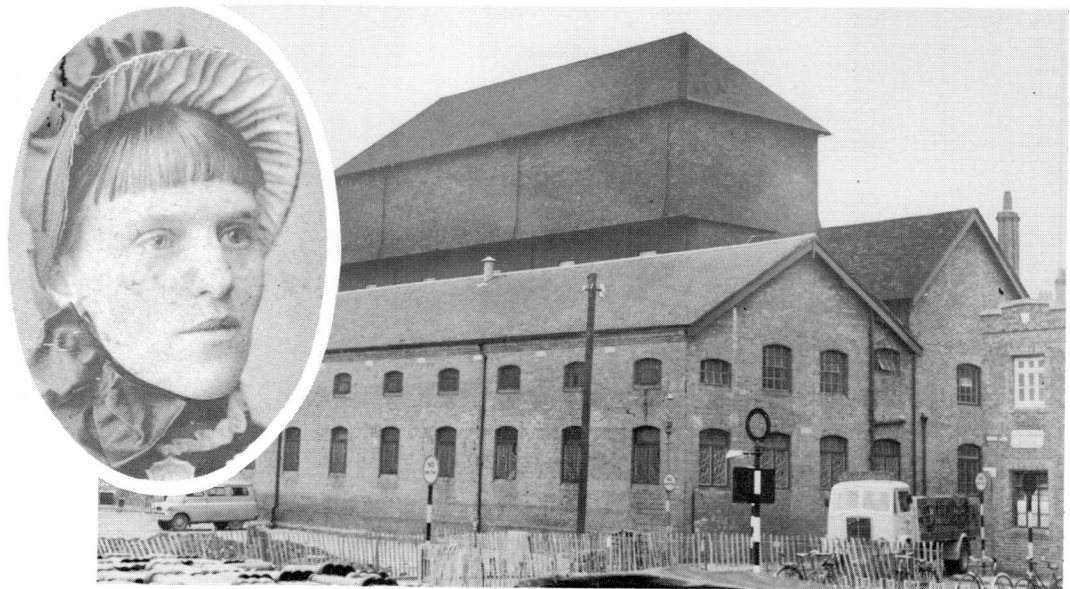

The era of conflict between beer and the bible finally passed after LEFT: the Wesleyan Church became High Street Methodist. RIGHT: The Roman Catholic Church and school of St Mary the Immaculate on the corner of Forlease Road and Bridge Street became a second hand goods shop. It has since been demolished, and BELOW: Nicholson's Brewery was replaced in our time by the new shopping precinct. INSET: The leading light of the temperance movement, Mrs Major Brown, one time leader of The Blue Ribbon Army.

INDEX

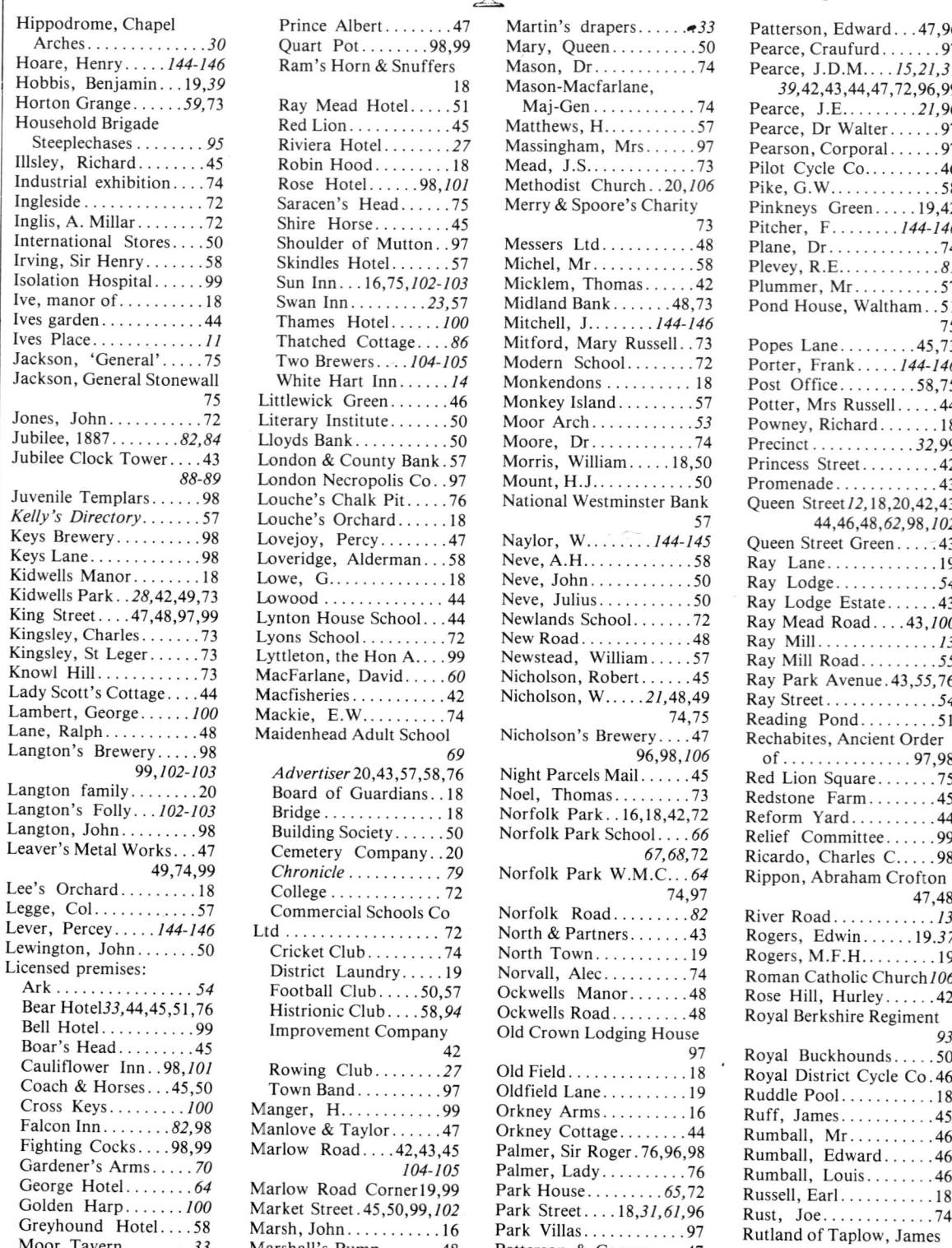

ENDPAPERS: Jubilee poster, 1887.

SUBSCRIBERS

Presentation Copies

1 **The Royal Borough of Windsor and Maidenhead**
2 **Berkshire County Council**
3 **Maidenhead Library**
4 **The Maidenhead Advertiser**

5	Tom Middleton	55	Mrs A. Bushnell	104	A.W. Valentine	152	M.D. Collins
6	Patricia Curtis	56	L. Bushnell	105	Clifford J. Bird	153	Mrs E.J. Johnson
7	Clive & Carolyn Birch	57	G.H. King	106	Mrs D.M. Houghton	154	D.I. Jackson
8	S.J. Roberts	58	William Alexander	107	Keith Wilsdon	155	Dr David J. Lloyd-Williams
9	T.H. Tilbury	59	Edward Sammes	108	Miss Pat Church		
10	Charles A. Yates	60	Peter & Pat Renk	109	G.P. Haythornthwaite	156	Mrs D.M. Pike
11	Baylis & Co	61	Bernard Mackrory	110	Michael Reade	157	Mr & Mrs W. Alexander
12	R.J. Cordon	62	J.C. Hunter	111	D.A. Lane		
13	L. Ainsworth	63	Lina & Mike Cole	112	Mrs H.C. Collins	158	Miss E. Rees
14	Mrs Elsie Jones	64	Mrs J. Nicholls	113	K.W. Elstow	159	P.T. Squire
15	S.T. Harmsworth	65	A. Kremenstein	114	I.D. & P.J. Terry	160	B.J. Huddart
16	P.R. Silverthorne	66	Mr & Mrs A. Woodcroft	115	John Challis	161	C.J. Townsend
17	Mrs W.I. Spickett			116	C.J. Sable	162	Mrs A. Holloway
18	Bryan E. Smith	67	J.J. Howorth	117	Miss A.J. Botley	163	Mrs B.E. Hepburn
19	N.W. Baylis	68	Mr & Mrs T. Stanley	118	Mrs White	164	Edward Brian Gibbons
20	Mrs K.M. Beckingham	69	Wg Cdr J.A.P. Owen	119	R.W. Clark		
21	Alan Kempton	70	James Calder	120	C.A.R. Cutler	165	Mrs A. Feldstein
22	K.W. Lovett	71	Mr & Mrs C.J. Grantham	121	J.H. Jeffries	166	Mrs Gillian Woodward
23	Margaret Jones	72	J.C. & G.I. Duncan	122	Mrs Elizabeth		
24 25	Norman Stribling	73	Mr & Mrs M.J. Jocock	123	O.B. Hart	167	L.J. Braitch
				124	M.D.Haeri	168	Mrs Charles Marks
26	K.J. Gallon	74	Miss P.H. Coleman	125	A.C. Ferguson	169	Mrs J. Russell
27	L.D. Higgs	75	M.J. Beardsmore	126	Mrs P. Bennett	170	J.S. Walker
28	J.C. Baskerville	76	Mrs R.G. Podalski	127	Mrs Gloria Blewitt	171	A.L. Walker
29	Veronica McGrath	77	T.J. Attree	128	Miss D.M. Robarts	172	Mrs J.S. Trigg
30	Jane Mercer	78	S.E. Fisher	129	Mrs P. Keating	173	Mrs B. McColm
31	Mrs C.K. Whitmore	79	G. Littleton	130	Mrs M.E. Andrews	174	L.J. Woodbridge
32	Mrs V.F. Bowie	80	Mrs Florence	131	Lady Liddell	175	D.P. Blow
33	Mrs D.M. Deeks	81	A.C.G. Smith	132	Mrs Brooke-Hitching	176	Mrs Iris Smith
34	F. Brooker	82	R. Newport	133	Mrs P.M. Curtis	177	Mrs Eileen
35	Mrs C.M. Peperell	83	K.C. Matthews	134	Stanley Coppins	178	C.A. Hutchings
36	Peter Chard	84	Ian Smallbone	135	H. Mills	179	W.S. Sampson
37	David Read	85	Eric John Wells	136	Mr & Mrs Derek Woolford	180	B.C. Lawrence
38	Malcolm Read	86	Mrs J. Hazell			181	Mr & Mrs R. Sambrook
39	Victoria & Albert Museum	87	Alwyn Greenhalgh	137	J. Wall		
		88	Anders R. Rumbold	138	Mrs Jean Giles	182	L.A. Dove
40	M.M. Crawford	89	F.B. Marmoy	139	D.J. Chuter	183	Miss D.M.S. Henry
41	Mrs R.F. Malpass	90	D.A. Hawes	140	Joss & Margaret Mullinger	184	Miss F.A. Tanser
42	Mrs Margaret G. Ratcliff	91	S.H. Plank			185	Robert C. Muller
		92	S. Loosen	141	Ann Hallworth	186	Mrs Jean Dawson
43 44	Miss Upson	93	Mr & Mrs Alan G. Poole	142	Mrs Johanna M. Raffan	187	H.A. Townsend
						188	Mrs M.E. Percy
45	Alec Davidson	94	Robert D. Watt	143	E.W. Fry	189	Chris Redknap
46	Alan Macrae	95	Mrs P.P. Rafter	144	Philip Edward John Scotcher	190	St Edmund's House
47	Janet Chown	96	A.F. Turner			191	Mrs D. Stewart
48	W.J.A. Watson	97	A.S. & J.E. Caldwell	145	Kenneth John Fry	192 193	G.P. Bennett
49	Victor C. Hill	98	M. & B. Johnston	146	Mrs J. Percy		
50	J.F. Perpy	99	Mrs P. Philpot	147	Mrs K.J.S. Phillips	194	Alwyn Greenhalgh
51	Mrs G. Rees	100	Elias Kupfermann	148	Mrs E.M. Bloomfield	195	Mrs Isabella Spriggs
52	D.A. Bay	101	Ron & Sally Ellis	149	Mrs Olive Petty	196	Mrs P.V. Walker
53	Mrs P.F. Jackson	102	D.J. Perry	150	Miss Joanna Mattingly	197	Vanessa B. Wood
54	J.F. Cox	103	Miss H. Higson			198	C. Marcus A. Wood
				151	R.G. Arnold	199	Muriel E. Wood

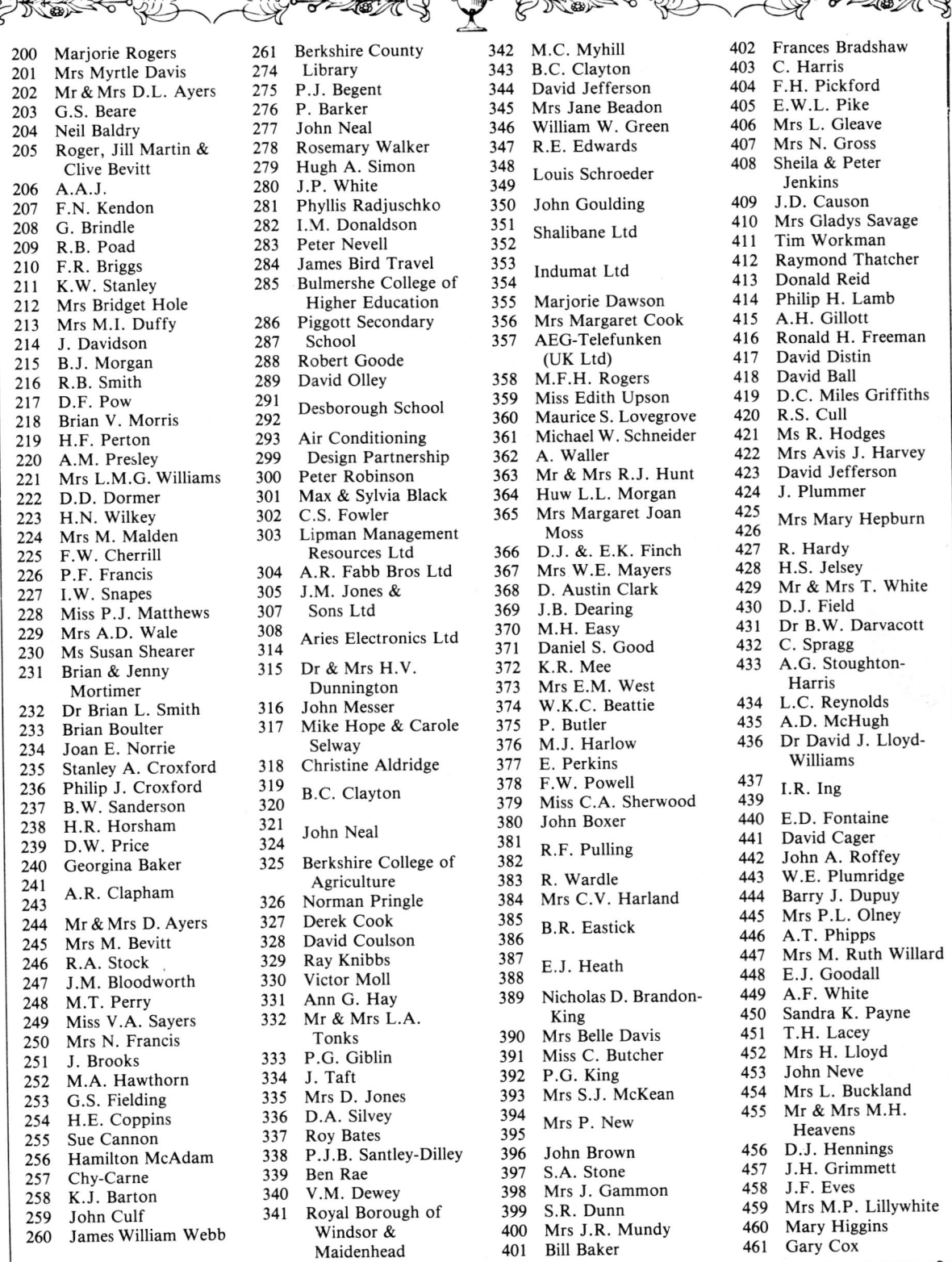

200	Marjorie Rogers	261	Berkshire County
201	Mrs Myrtle Davis	274	Library
202	Mr & Mrs D.L. Ayers	275	P.J. Begent
203	G.S. Beare	276	P. Barker
204	Neil Baldry	277	John Neal
205	Roger, Jill Martin &	278	Rosemary Walker
	Clive Bevitt	279	Hugh A. Simon
206	A.A.J.	280	J.P. White
207	F.N. Kendon	281	Phyllis Radjuschko
208	G. Brindle	282	I.M. Donaldson
209	R.B. Poad	283	Peter Nevell
210	F.R. Briggs	284	James Bird Travel
211	K.W. Stanley	285	Bulmershe College of
212	Mrs Bridget Hole		Higher Education
213	Mrs M.I. Duffy	286	Piggott Secondary
214	J. Davidson	287	School
215	B.J. Morgan	288	Robert Goode
216	R.B. Smith	289	David Olley
217	D.F. Pow	291	
218	Brian V. Morris	292	Desborough School
219	H.F. Perton	293	Air Conditioning
220	A.M. Presley	299	Design Partnership
221	Mrs L.M.G. Williams	300	Peter Robinson
222	D.D. Dormer	301	Max & Sylvia Black
223	H.N. Wilkey	302	C.S. Fowler
224	Mrs M. Malden	303	Lipman Management
225	F.W. Cherrill		Resources Ltd
226	P.F. Francis	304	A.R. Fabb Bros Ltd
227	I.W. Snapes	305	J.M. Jones &
228	Miss P.J. Matthews	307	Sons Ltd
229	Mrs A.D. Wale	308	Aries Electronics Ltd
230	Ms Susan Shearer	314	
231	Brian & Jenny	315	Dr & Mrs H.V.
	Mortimer		Dunnington
232	Dr Brian L. Smith	316	John Messer
233	Brian Boulter	317	Mike Hope & Carole
234	Joan E. Norrie		Selway
235	Stanley A. Croxford	318	Christine Aldridge
236	Philip J. Croxford	319	B.C. Clayton
237	B.W. Sanderson	320	
238	H.R. Horsham	321	John Neal
239	D.W. Price	324	
240	Georgina Baker	325	Berkshire College of
241	A.R. Clapham		Agriculture
243		326	Norman Pringle
244	Mr & Mrs D. Ayers	327	Derek Cook
245	Mrs M. Bevitt	328	David Coulson
246	R.A. Stock	329	Ray Knibbs
247	J.M. Bloodworth	330	Victor Moll
248	M.T. Perry	331	Ann G. Hay
249	Miss V.A. Sayers	332	Mr & Mrs L.A.
250	Mrs N. Francis		Tonks
251	J. Brooks	333	P.G. Giblin
252	M.A. Hawthorn	334	J. Taft
253	G.S. Fielding	335	Mrs D. Jones
254	H.E. Coppins	336	D.A. Silvey
255	Sue Cannon	337	Roy Bates
256	Hamilton McAdam	338	P.J.B. Santley-Dilley
257	Chy-Carne	339	Ben Rae
258	K.J. Barton	340	V.M. Dewey
259	John Culf	341	Royal Borough of
260	James William Webb		Windsor &
			Maidenhead

342	M.C. Myhill	402	Frances Bradshaw
343	B.C. Clayton	403	C. Harris
344	David Jefferson	404	F.H. Pickford
345	Mrs Jane Beadon	405	E.W.L. Pike
346	William W. Green	406	Mrs L. Gleave
347	R.E. Edwards	407	Mrs N. Gross
348	Louis Schroeder	408	Sheila & Peter
349			Jenkins
350	John Goulding	409	J.D. Causon
351	Shalibane Ltd	410	Mrs Gladys Savage
352		411	Tim Workman
353	Indumat Ltd	412	Raymond Thatcher
354		413	Donald Reid
355	Marjorie Dawson	414	Philip H. Lamb
356	Mrs Margaret Cook	415	A.H. Gillott
357	AEG-Telefunken	416	Ronald H. Freeman
	(UK Ltd)	417	David Distin
358	M.F.H. Rogers	418	David Ball
359	Miss Edith Upson	419	D.C. Miles Griffiths
360	Maurice S. Lovegrove	420	R.S. Cull
361	Michael W. Schneider	421	Ms R. Hodges
362	A. Waller	422	Mrs Avis J. Harvey
363	Mr & Mrs R.J. Hunt	423	David Jefferson
364	Huw L.L. Morgan	424	J. Plummer
365	Mrs Margaret Joan	425	Mrs Mary Hepburn
	Moss	426	
366	D.J. & E.K. Finch	427	R. Hardy
367	Mrs W.E. Mayers	428	H.S. Jelsey
368	D. Austin Clark	429	Mr & Mrs T. White
369	J.B. Dearing	430	D.J. Field
370	M.H. Easy	431	Dr B.W. Darvacott
371	Daniel S. Good	432	C. Spragg
372	K.R. Mee	433	A.G. Stoughton-
373	Mrs E.M. West		Harris
374	W.K.C. Beattie	434	L.C. Reynolds
375	P. Butler	435	A.D. McHugh
376	M.J. Harlow	436	Dr David J. Lloyd-
377	E. Perkins		Williams
378	F.W. Powell	437	I.R. Ing
379	Miss C.A. Sherwood	439	
380	John Boxer	440	E.D. Fontaine
381	R.F. Pulling	441	David Cager
382		442	John A. Roffey
383	R. Wardle	443	W.E. Plumridge
384	Mrs C.V. Harland	444	Barry J. Dupuy
385	B.R. Eastick	445	Mrs P.L. Olney
386		446	A.T. Phipps
387	E.J. Heath	447	Mrs M. Ruth Willard
388		448	E.J. Goodall
389	Nicholas D. Brandon-	449	A.F. White
	King	450	Sandra K. Payne
390	Mrs Belle Davis	451	T.H. Lacey
391	Miss C. Butcher	452	Mrs H. Lloyd
392	P.G. King	453	John Neve
393	Mrs S.J. McKean	454	Mrs L. Buckland
394	Mrs P. New	455	Mr & Mrs M.H.
395			Heavens
396	John Brown	456	D.J. Hennings
397	S.A. Stone	457	J.H. Grimmett
398	Mrs J. Gammon	458	J.F. Eves
399	S.R. Dunn	459	Mrs M.P. Lillywhite
400	Mrs J.R. Mundy	460	Mary Higgins
401	Bill Baker	461	Gary Cox

462	T.A. Gillis	487 H.R. Clay	513 James Stracham	538 Miss Sheila Thornton

462 T.A. Gillis
463 R. Wood
464 J.E. Norrie
465 Mrs M. Merrill
466 Mrs J.A. Smart
467 Mary Bradley
468 L.J. Newman
469 Mrs S.E. Bennett
470 Mrs E. Gordon
471
472 Graham E. Cooper
473 O.J. Miles
474 Mrs D.R. Eales
475 D.G. Smith
476 Martin Parks
477 H.W. Thomas & Son
478
479 K.I. Saunders
480 Miss D.E. Smith
481 E.L. Bond
482 Mrs M. Tassie
483 S.A. Stone
484 H.E. Wilkins
485 D.W. Mason
486 Mrs P. Durham

487 H.R. Clay
488 Mrs I.K. Baker
489 Mrs A. Whitehead
490 Ronald Leslie Jewell
491 A.R. Bezant
492 Brian A. Beard
493 Nicholas G. Winton
496
497 R. Munns
498 Mary Cox
499 Mrs L.E. Cooper
500 N.A. Hunt
501 Holyport C of E
    Primary School
502 Mrs Gay Seguro
503 Olive Tait
504 Dr D.R.C. Bell
505 Carole L. Rennie
506 Christopher G. Ketley
507 Roger J. Strike
508 D.F. Dunning
509 Pat & Derek Taylor
510 Miss Barbara Bassil
511 Dr K.R. Pal
512 Clifford Webb

513 James Stracham
514 Mrs. P.H. Freer
515 R.L. Gosnell
516 J.F. Mason
517 C.W. Watson
518 G.F. Brainch
519 A.R.F. Cook
520 C.J. Ware
521 J. Morgan
522 J.W. Portsmouth
523 R.T. Brisley
524 W.A. King
525 P.J. Povey
526 T.E. Oliver
527 T.F. Sandalls
528 J. Hawes
529 A.J.A. Woollard
530 R.C. Tapley
531 Miss A. Middleditch
532 A.L. Hall
533 C. Lambourne
534 C. Crowe
535 H.J. Farr
536 Mrs M.I. Paddick
537 Miss Patricia Beckley

538 Miss Sheila Thornton
539 Mrs M. Weston
540 J. Cowley
541 Mrs Moore
542 Mrs M. Brill
543 Mrs S. Webb
544 Mrs L.M. Allan
545 Mrs P.M. Sheader
546 Billie Tideman
547 Mrs E.J. Lewis
548 Mr & Mrs B.J.
    Mantle
549 G.W. Russell
550 Mrs L.F. Barlow
551 Mrs D.A. Stone
552 Miss I. Adkins
553 I.J. Over
554 Mrs A. Ashton
555 Mrs D. Evans
556 Mrs R. Dunn
557 Desborough School
    Library

Remaining names unlisted

*As the Victorian era drew to a close, the Jubilee typified yesterday's town,
Maidenhead in 1887—riverside revellers and industrious traders take tea to
a background of martial airs, flags aflying, hats on heads, in the sunshine
of their virtues and midst the greenery of Grenfell Park.*

MANIE TUNEFULLE BANDES OF MUSICIANERS

Shal entertaine ye populace, and ye Lasses and Lads shal be bidden to join in ye Mazy Dance to ye straines of righte joyouse musike, and to celebrate on ye Greene and Spryngie Turfe ye Ancient Mysteries of 'Droppe ye Kerchief,' of "Kisse in ye Rynge," and manie other righte merrie games.

Atte ye Houre of Three by ye Clok and thereafter until ye daylighte shal fayle, there shal be open in —— YE CRYCKET FIELDE——

A FANCY FAYRE

Wherein will be Brave Showes of manie and divers kindes—to wit :

MAISTER RICHARDSON'S BOOTHE,

Wherein atte 3, 4, 5, 6, 7, and 8 of ye Clok—will be sette forth ye Romantic Drama of Thrylynge Interest, written by Maister Byron, and yclept

"ABANDONDINO YE BLOODLESSE,"

CHARACTERS:

Abandondino -	- - -	-	Bye Maister Micawber Macbethe.
Mysteriouse Individual	- - -	-	Bye ye Man from ye Moone,
Two Cocks (who do crowe)	-	-	-

To be followed each tyme bye

——Ye favourite Domestic Drama (lykewyse bye Maister Byron) yclept——

"YE ROSEBUD OF STINGINGNETTLE FARM,"

Or "Ye Villainous Squire and ye Virtuous Villager."

CHARACTERS:

Caffer Turmutfield -	-	(ye Yeoman Farmer)	-	-	Bye Maister Irving Barrette.